Dermot Earley
AN OFFICER AND
A GENTLEMAN

JOHN SCALLY

Ballpoint Press

Published in 2014 by Ballpoint Press
4 Wyndham Park, Bray, Co Wicklow, Republic of Ireland.
Telephone: 00353 86 821 7631
Email: ballpointpress1@gmail.com
Web: www.ballpointpress.com

ISBN 978-0-9926732-3-9

Book design and production by Elly Design

Cover photograph: Dermot Earley in action for Roscomming in July, 1985.
© INPHO/Billy Stickland

Printed and bound by GraphyCems

Contents

Foreword

By Dermot Earley Junior

A PHOTO album of Irish soldiers who served with the United Nations Interim Force in Lebanon lies on the coffee table of Walter's Barber Shop in Tibnine, South Lebanon. In January 2014, while serving with the 42nd Infantry Group, not far from Tibnine, I visited the shop. While perusing through the album I noticed Dad's Mass card was placed where a photo once was. I knew exactly the photo that used to be in the album and it was the reason I made the trip to Walter's; it was taken in 1997 when my father was the Commanding Officer of the 81st Infantry Battalion based in Camp Shamrock, Tibnine, and it was at home on my mantelpiece in Newbridge.

The photo was of Dad sitting in the barber's chair. What was special about it was that it captured him perfectly, in his essence, in his prime, full of life, fit, tanned from the Lebanese sun and smiling from ear to ear. The photo was discovered by an army officer serving there in 2011, borrowed from Walter, brought home to Ireland and given to Lt Gen Sean McCann former Chief of Staff of the Defence Forces. He made a number of copies and gave them to our family. After introducing myself to Walter his eyes lit up and he spoke of my father with fond memories and great admiration before enthusiastically enquiring as to where his photo was.

It wasn't until the 9th of May 2014 that I was able to return to Walter's and as soon as I set foot inside the door he asked, "where is my photo?" It is now proudly back in the photo album adorning Walter's coffee table in Tibnine, South Lebanon. Just one example of the impact Dad had on people throughout the course of his short but distinguished life, both far and wide, including those not brought up in the traditions of the GAA, who never saw him grace Hyde Park on Connaught Final Day, who may never have heard of Roscommon, but knew they were in the presence of someone special.

I pen this foreword with sadness as my father should be writing this. It is four years since Dad's passing on the 23rd of June 2010. The Defence Forces lost a great leader, the GAA lost a legend, Roscommon lost a son and we lost a husband, father and grandfather. His story was told up until 1992 but in the pages ahead you will see he had much more to say, our only regret is that it will be told posthumously through the legacy he left behind, the impact he had on people, their story through his influence, and conversations he had with John Scally.

Only one man could write his biography and we want to especially thank John Scally for his friendship, his vision, his encouragement and his enthusiasm in taking on this challenge. I know Dad would be enormously proud that his legacy continues to live on through John's words and the Earley family are enormously proud too.

Finally, Dad would also be particularly pleased that all the royalties from the book will go to charities that he had an interest in.

Dermot Earley Junior
August 2014

Prologue

I WAS scared, I was scared, tired and unprepared . . .

Chris Martin's words from his Coldplay song had just taken on a new significance for me. I stared at my hand in my lap, clasped so tightly the knuckles had turned a translucent white. But I felt the shock in my blood, actually felt it pumping and churning inside me. I had never known anything like it. I just wanted things back the way they used to be.

The sentence stung. It was as though I had been cut, the knife having gone so deep that the wound was not yet painful, it produced merely shock. It seemed to me after that conversation that the world was thoroughly altered. It was not something you could explain adequately, why it was that everything was folly. So much of what excited people in normal life seemed wholly and disturbingly petty.

An almost Proustian pang of memory came over me as I remembered all his glory days in the Roscommon jersey. I could not remember time looping in on itself in such a manner before, when life had been measured out in minutes rather than in hours and a sadness so deep that no tears could come.

It was the Saturday before Christmas in 2009. Dermot had just told me about the illness that would claim his life six months later. His words were full of positivity about the prognosis but the uncharacteristic weakness in his voice told another story.

A nurse with blonde hair peered anxiously as he walked unsteadily down the corridor. He smiled faintly uncomfortable with the slight strain of sociability, drenched by reminiscences that seemed to have no regard for circumstances or place. Earlier that day the doctor glanced over him with an expression of faint alarm. He raised his eyes and saw it all in an instant over Dermot's face. Love. Family. Responsibility. All to be lost? These things Dermot understood instinctively. He never gave them voice, not even within the privacy of his thoughts.

A pilgrim's progress

Dermot's funeral will live with me forever - looking down on a gathering for an occasion almost unbearably sad: a centre of my life gone. I was near to tears and in my heart there was something stirring, a sense of outrage, a feeling of total despair. I could not bring myself to think of him in the past tense but I had seen the evidence of the previous night as he lay in his coffin. I hoped fervently his soul had been set free from its anguish and that he would find peace at last in a higher, more perfect world. There was no strain anymore, and the features of his face were calm, now that he had been released from the struggle for breath.

As I walked with John MacKenna to the graveyard after Dermot's funeral, in a scene sculpted in sadness, the emptiness I felt pervaded everything and I found I couldn't put my thoughts away and I began to understand how I would miss my great friend. Like a hidden grieving that rises to grab the heart, my soul was ambushed with old emotions, and my lips began to tremble, and for a brief instant I was swept into the current of all that I had lost.

Katy Dobey's poem 'Sestina' captures the loss I feel for a great friend:

The great distance, the delayed absence,
That causes this inscrutable pain,
That injures my heart with one blow.

Yet as I travelled home I knew that despite the tragic circumstances of Dermot's death my life was greatly enriched by such a man. Nobody did more than him to make the sport I love so well the beautiful game. My mind flashed back to a November day in 1991, a day so wet even the puddles had waves in them, when Dermot shook my hand for the first time. Legend had it that when he shook your hand it was shook forever. I recalled the immediate authority that draped itself over his face in the Curragh that day.

Then there was his voice that I would hear no more. I

remembered how quickly I learned not just to listen to the words he had used, but tones in which I could distinguish delicacy, irony and compassion. I wondered why God could allow the premature sacrifice of such wealth. Life is full of riddles that only the dead can answer.

Heaven Knows No Frontiers

For 130 years the GAA has been the one fixed point in a fast changing age. Those years have not been without their troubles but even when the storm clouds gathered the people's organisation has not withered before their blast and a greener, better, stronger movement lay in the sunshine when the tempest was past. Our economic system values measurable outcomes but what is deepest about us, transcends what can be said and outstrips what can be analysed. It is not given to us to peer into the mysteries of the future but we can safely predict that in the coming 130 years Gaelic Games continue to reach to something profound within us. For what, we may not always be sure - except that there are moments when we know that there is more to life – and to us – than the grim and grasping existence of seeking and striving and succeeding. There are moments of wonder, hope and grace that give us hints of ecstasy and lift us out of ourselves. They are, in Yeats's phrase, 'the soul's monuments of its own magnificence'. These moments take us to the heart of the deep mystery of being a person, the subterranean stirrings of the spirit, the rapid rhythms of the human heart. They have to do with remembering who we are, enlarging our perspective, seeing ourselves whole.

Dermot was a hero in the true sense of the term because when he performed well, *do lioigh an laoch san uile dhuine* (the hero in all of us was exulted). I was forcefully reminded of that after Roscommon's 2010 famous Connacht final victory over Sligo.

That evening I received a text from Roscommon's midfielder Karol Mannion who had played a pivotal role in that victory which simply said: 'We did it for Dermot.'

From the dawn of time identification with heroes has been an integral part of the human condition. Great sporting performances have always grabbed the imagination of the young of all ages as they fantasize about emulating the glorious feats of their heroes. Thanks in no small part to television sports heroes occupy an even larger part of the imagination than in earlier generations. William Butler Yeats exhorted people to go to their graves empty, having not wasted a moment of their lives. Dermot need have no worries on that score. It is given to few mortals to become eternally remembered after their stint in this vale of tears is over, even fewer as a consequence of their achievements on the GAA fields. With the passing years names like Christy Ring and Seán Purcell have an even stronger evocative power: they are a chant, an invocation, a beckoning magic for fans. Dermot belongs in such elite company. He will forever remain a true Roscommon icon.

All football fans in Roscommon, Kildare and beyond are the curators of Dermot's memories.

A vein of grief runs through my life now. I have made the discovery that grief could attach itself with permanence. It attached itself and then it burrowed inside and made a nest and lingered like an unwelcome guest. It ate whatever was warm in the chambers of the heart, and then the coldness settled in permanently. This is the wound that never really heals but each in our own unique way learns to live with it, with greater or lesser success.

Death ends a life but not a relationship. Memory becomes your partner. You nurture it. You hold it. You dance with it.

Four years on Dermot's absence has become a presence. It was one of the great blessings of my life to become his biographer. My greatest blessing though was to have been his friend for 20 years. As a result I don't cry any longer because it is over but smile because it happened.

The life of the dead is placed in the memories of the living. The love we feel in life keeps people alive beyond their time. Anyone who has given love will always live on in another's heart. The stars in the sky are not the eyes of God but the stars of those who have passed on lovingly watching over us. Dermot's star will shine the brightest for those who loved him.

Goodbye to you my trusted friend.

Introduction

THE inspiration for this book, albeit completely unintentionally, was Mary Earley. While Dermot was managing Roscommon in particular he would always be very cautious in interviews with the media before a game, even ones he would be most confident of winning. Mary would from time to time get frustrated at his pronouncements and told him he should cast off his inhibitions and say exactly what he believed. Knowing that for every manager who has boldly stated their convictions in public like Ger Loughnane's, 'We're going to do it' there have been comments like Babs Keating's, 'Donkeys don't win derbies', which have come back to bite them in the ass.

When you spent even a few moments in the company of Dermot you were immediately conscious of the fact that you are in the presence of what the Irish rugby coach Joe Schmidt calls 'contagious integrity'. He was a very self-effacing man, perhaps too much so for his own good; yet this was often a restraint passing unrecognised as a hidden strength, intended for the good of others. Even so, there were times when we saw that observant eye register just a faint shadow of irony with just a flicker.

In relaxed conversation he could be amazingly open, but in public was much more guarded because he was always conscious of his duty to his various offices. An unflagging loyalty to his profession and its principles had made him, over the years, increasingly considered in his speech and actions, and evermore exacting regarding the truth in even his most casual reportage. It was a sort of black joke he shared with himself.

Dermot was always acutely sensitive about his position in the army as well as his various roles in the GAA but Mary's comments struck a chord and it did sow the seed of writing down his thoughts in a second book after we worked on his biography in 1992. Initially the project was going to be a book about the army and the GAA to mark the 125th anniversary of the GAA in 2009. It quickly emerged that Dermot had strong views about a number of issues in the GAA and beyond and the idea of doing a second book with him was born, which would in the main take up the story where are our first book had finished in 1992. However, from my point of point of view some of the ways he reappraised his earlier career from the first book was equally interesting.

While he was the Chief of Staff of the Defence Forces he felt too constrained from airing all his views in public so we had provisionally fixed the year after his retirement as a publication date when finally he could air his views more publicly.

Sadly Dermot's illness intervened in the interim and this became a biography not the autobiography we had planned. The fantasy ending for the book was with Dermot Junior winning the All-Ireland medal that eluded his father but real life seldom provides the fairytale finale we so desire.

Dermot's great legacy is the six children that he and his wife Mary were so proud of but hopefully this book will be a legacy for his grandchildren.

I am very glad he is part of my life. An entire county has cause to say the same.

1

No Blood On Their Hands

I HAD hundreds of conversations with Dermot Earley on the phone, in the course of a close friendship of 20 years, but three stand out – two during his illness and one the morning after he was sacked as Roscommon manager.

Results were disappointing during his two-year tenure and a significant amount of Roscommon fans were vociferous in their criticism of his performance. Things came to a head with the defeat to John O'Mahony's Leitrim by a point in the Connacht Championship in 1994. Although Leitrim went on to win only their second provincial title that year, the rumblings of discontent among Roscommon fans grew to a crescendo.

The day after Dermot's death in the course of an effusive tribute Shannonside radio's leading personality Joe Finnegan recalled on his morning show:

'His playing days with Roscommon were unforgettable but afterwards his time as manager, he'd probably be the first to admit himself, didn't go well. I couldn't get over the treatment he got in certain quarters. Some of it was vicious and they couldn't get rid of him fast enough. I remember thinking at the time: My God if they can do this to Dermot Earley, what will they do to somebody else?'

Some weeks after the Leitrim game, Dermot met up with two senior officials on the Roscommon County Board to review his stewardship of the team. As attention to detail was his mantra, Dermot had prepared a meticulous plan for the coming year. When he was asked at the start of the meeting what he thought about things, Dermot launched into his plan with his customary enthusiasm but he quickly noticed that the two men did not seem to be really listening and were looking at each other rather than at him. He came to an abrupt halt and asked them bluntly: 'Do you want me to resign?'

One replied: 'Well, would you?'

Thus ended his managerial career with the county he loved so well.

Knowing about the meeting I rang him the next morning. It was not like a Roy Keane and Alex Ferguson situation after United let Keano go. There was no bitterness or rancour. However, the conversation was memorable for the amount of uncharacteristic pauses and because it was the only time I ever heard him sounding clearly hurt, not even during his illness was there a hint of that tone. Nobody likes getting rejected and dumped by one of the few great loves of their life.

Ours is an age when the currency is a loyalty bonus. Dermot never sought such a bonus but instead wanted to give the bonus of loyalty to Roscommon.

The way the meeting had been conducted was not the way he would have handled it himself. Twenty years on his summary sentence, said not in anger but in a soft whisper of resignation, remains indelibly carved on my memory:

'They wanted my head on a plate but they didn't want my blood on their hands.'

2

Managerial Moments

FOOTBALL management is not rocket science. It is a lot more complicated and demanding. Gaelic football managers can be classified into two categories: those who have been sacked and those who will be sacked. There can be a fine line when a manager's admirable independence of mind spills over into self-destructive stubbornness. Think of Jack Charlton's treatment of David O'Leary.

The manager is doomed to betray the hopes and ambitions of his fans. He is always a flawed hero who, even after extraordinary achievement, can exit on a note that reveals his human frailty. The manager is permanently in limbo, the laws of statistics always catch up with him. Defeat, like guilt, refines the methods of self-torture, threading the beads of detail into an eternal loop, a rosary to be fingered for a lifetime and maybe even beyond. Dermot Earley was destined to learn this lesson the hard way.

In 1992 he was offered the job of managing the Roscommon team. After consultations with Mary, he turned the job down fearing the price on his family life would be too high. He was given a week to reconsider.

The next evening he was driving his oldest daughter, Paula, to a camoige match. Paula was aware of the situation in relation to his managerial opportunity. She inquired if her father would be taking the position. The question was turned around and she was asked what her opinion was. She said: "Oh Daddy, it would be great."

Much taken aback by her enthusiasm for his acceptance of the job his five other children were consulted and they were equally enthusiastic. Not for the first time, especially in relation to the Roscommon team, the heart ruled the head and he reversed his position and accepted the offer.

Despite Mary's reservations, Dermot was energised by a sense of the possibilities of a job. Subsequent events would cloud the memories, but the fact was that it was rather like that Christmas morning sensation of being about to give a present that would give delight and joy to the whole family. Sleep would not come that night, or came only in quick plunges from which he emerged, giddy with thoughts he could not choose or direct. In the deserts of the heart he was pumped up with a childish feeling of abandonment. The fact that scarcely any of his Connacht compatriots gave them a chance of winning Sam Maguire within 12 months was not a concern for him.

Dermot was an ardent disciple of the school of positive thinking. One of his favourite stories to stress the message of 'having a go' was about Brendan Behan. The great writer was being interviewed on Canadian television and was clearly under the influence. The irate interviewer asked him bluntly how he could have the temerity to be drunk on live television. Behan replied: 'I was sitting in a pub in Dublin last week and I saw a beer mat which said: "Drink Canada dry." So when I got here I said I would give it a go.'

Come on the Rossies

Roscommon is a land without royalty but when it comes to football Dermot Earley was, is and always will be king. Danny Murray, the only Roscommon footballer to win All-Star awards in consecutive years, described him as 'the Pele of Gaelic football'. As a player, Gaelic football provided an ideal context in which to express his combination of cerebral gifts and extreme competitiveness. The football field was an exhilarating arena where he could put his abilities and his nerve against those of everyone else - and only the best-equipped would survive. He wanted a theatre and here was one ready-made for him, with all the elements for testing himself already created and a marvellously varied and endlessly fascinating characters. His achievements as a player were not enough in themselves to warrant confidence, given the number of great players who have not successfully made the transition to inter-county management.

Within Roscommon there was an unspoken question after his appointment as manager. There were no questions about his subtlety, verve, sophistication, refinement and versatility of technique or of his profound understanding of how skill, perception and speed should be deployed, but a nagging doubt lingered. Had he the stomach to trade in a rougher currency if the circumstances arose?

He went into the job with his eyes open:

'I am a big fan of Con Houlinhan: the man, the myth and the journalist. I love his flair for words. I especially like Con's powers of observation on the way Irish public opinion moves like a flock of starlings: all veering one way in a great cloud before suddenly turning and going together in the opposite direction. I knew that any credit I had in the bank from my days as a Roscommon player would quickly run out if the results went against me. I also knew that the County Board would be calling me also.'

Supermac

In the main we remember not the scores and the results in latter years. It is the great players who linger in our minds, in our imagination. Dermot's arrival as manager coincided with the departure of one of the giants of Roscommon football:

'Tony McManus had just retired. His loss was incalculable. He was deservedly chosen on the Connacht team of the Millennium. He was a class act.

'I particularly valued his intelligence. I remember passing a ball to Tony's brother Eamonn during a league match in Hyde Park against Dublin where we were struggling to get a narrow victory. Eamonn was running away from the goal. If I had passed to him directly he would have had to continue running away from the goal and then turn, wasting valuable time. So, I passed the ball inside to him. I am sure that he thought it was a bad pass, not realising that there was no Dublin player near. As he turned, the ball bounced before him and all he had to do was to tap it over the bar. He acknowledged the pass and the game went on. At the end of the game Tony was the man who complimented me. He had seen what was involved and knew it was a great pass.

'He is the sort of player who comes along once in every generation if you are lucky – especially in a county with the population the size of Roscommon. He had been the conductor of the orchestra for years but there was no one to take the baton from him.

'I was fortunate to have Gay Sheeran at my disposal from the 1980 team. He was one of Roscommon's greatest goalies of all time. He brought experience into the dressing-room and is a great character, a wonderful storyteller and amazing company. I know many people will not understand this but the bond I felt and still feel for the players on the county team is much stronger than I do for lads I meet every day now. The reason for it is very simple; I spent so much time with them.

'My only problem with Gay is that he always makes me feel a lot older than I thought. He tells of a match on a wet day and Dermot Washington was wearing only one glove. Dermot was called after me which is both flattering and ageing in itself. The conversation between them unfolded as follows:

Gay: "You're like Jimmy Mannion. He would always wear only one glove."

Dermot: "Who's Jimmy Mannion?"

Gay: "How can you not know Jimmy Mannion? He was on the Roscommon team that won the Connacht final in 1972 and got to the League final in 1974."

Dermot: "I wasn't born in 1974."'

'Gay was a great asset but we haven't seen Tony's like since. I was thrilled when Roscommon won the All-Ireland minor title in 2006 and was especially excited by watching Donie Shine, particularly as I had played with his Dad, because I thought at last here is someone who has the potential to fill Tony's shoes.

'As a manager you try and plan for every eventuality but there will always be curved balls coming at you. Tony McManus missed out on a great chance to win a Connacht final in 1986, when through his work as a vet he contracted Brucellosis. No manager can anticipate that. The one constant worry though is injuries and some players you worry about more than others in this respect. The one forward who really could have taken on a leadership role with the forwards from Tony was my brother Paul but injuries were hamstringing him, if you will pardon the pun, and he had to retire prematurely. If I had a fully fit Paul or Tony I genuinely believe we would have won silverware - but there are no medals for "if onlys".'

Building blocks

Failure will always dog the most successful stride. To that end the great managers are often not easy men. They have to be driven by an endless quest to avoid the inevitable, to minimize risks and to maximize potential. The will to win is easy but the will to prepare to win is more problematic for many players.

Increasingly sport is becoming identified with the culture of the survival of the fittest. This involves subordinating everything else in sport to winning. This approach was encapsulated in the popular saying attributed to the famous American coach, Vince Lombardi, 'Winning isn't all-important, it's the only thing.' Only winners would survive. This is easier said than done and it required a manager with an ability to look at the match from the perspective of the way the whole team was playing and simultaneously to conceptualize ways to foil the opposition's game plan. Not all players would immediately see this bigger picture.

In the old days: win or die was the code; arousing the player's anger. That kind of approach, though it often gets the blood boiling, interferes with concentration and may ultimately backfire. Earley appreciated the fine line between playing hard and playing angry. When individual players were matched up against someone with superior skills the message was, 'We'll give you any help but you're going to have to be the door that doesn't open.' Sometimes a few words like that were all that was needed.

A recent example of such a ploy came when Joe Schmidt managed Leinster. The team had suffered a defeat, put in a poor performance and got a hammering in the press, and another game was looming the following weekend, with morale as low as he had ever seen it. Leo Cullen came up with an idea, or basically an order, where every player was assigned a player they had to send a text to. It had to be a positive text, about something the recipient did really well. Schmidt was unsure about the idea, but it worked wonders. The following day morale was back sky high, and they put in a powerhouse performance that weekend.

The boss

A wide variety of attributes come together like converging lines in the good coach. The American football coach, Walter Gillet once offered a definition:

'A coach is a politician, a judge, a public speaker, a teacher, a trainer, a financier, a labourer, a psychologist, a psychiatrist, and a chaplain. He must be an optimist and yet at times appear to be a pessimist, seem humble and yet seem very proud, strong but at times weak, confident yet not overconfident, enthusiastic but not too enthusiastic.

'He must have the hide of an elephant, the fierceness of a lion, the pep of a young pup, the guts of an ox, the stamina of an antelope, the wisdom of an owl, the cunning of a fox, and the heart of a kitten.

'He must be willing to give freely of his time, his money, his energy, his youth, his family life, and his health. In return he must expect little if any financial reward, little comfort on earth, little praise but plenty of criticism.

'However, a good coach is respected and is a leader in his

community, is loved by his team, and makes lasting friends wherever he goes.

'He has the satisfaction of seeing young people develop and improve in ability. He learns the thrill of victory and how to accept defeat with grace. His associations with athletes help keep him young in mind and spirit, and he too must grow and improve in ability with his team.

'In his heart he knows that, in spite of the inconvenience, the criticism, and the demands on his time, he loves his work, for he is the coach.'

Earley was acutely aware that the coach with all these laudable attributes is a mirage. His university of life was to a significant extent the university of sport, and it had taught him many invaluable lessons because the values so inherent within the game apply equally to every walk of life: respect the past, but not be imprisoned by its traditions.

He did have some initial plans to implement. Any squad is like a fine plant. If it is to bloom year after year, it requires prudent pruning by a skilled hand. The GAA refuse tip has been overflowing with talented but complex characters who, with sensitive, imaginative handling could have produced so much more and not have faded into oblivion at such an early stage of their careers.

Earley choose a player to illustrate this point - a phenomenon capable of reducing the best and swiftest defenders to impotent pursuit, of leaving them as miserable stragglers baffled by astonishing surges of acceleration and devastatingly sudden changes of direction:

'In my years playing with Roscommon, the most exciting player we ever had was John O'Connor (whose son Darrach is now playing with Donegal). Jigger could do things others wouldn't even dream of. He could do flicks and weaves that would electrify the fans and could chip in some great scores. When he was on fire like the All-Ireland semi-final against Kerry in 1978 he was virtually unmarkable – though I think Jimmy Deenihan left quite a few marks on his jersey that day! We had played well in midfield and in attack in the Connacht final against Galway and won well but we were unable to reproduce that form against Kerry – except Jigger and in many ways he seemed to carry the fight to them on his own at times.

'Jigger was a special talent and a one-off. He had the talent to be one of the greats of the game outside Roscommon, where he rightly remains a much-loved figure, but he had a temperament that need to be carefully nurtured. What would work with most of the rest of us would not work with Jigger and he need to be managed in a unique way. Likewise Mick Finneran was as skilful a player as I ever played with but drudgery in training was not to his taste so he too needed to be handled differently. Neither of them had the long glittering careers their talent merited and I had learned the lesson from seeing them at first hand that a one size fits all approach to management was not good enough.'

Unlike Heinz, football managers come in more than 57 varieties. Great squads are not constructed only on the training field, but in every circumstance where the squad can grow together as a group of people who genuinely care about each other and enjoy each other's company. Each player affects the other and the other affects the next, and each player is full of stories, but in a united team the stories are all one. The squad form a society of their own outside the common hierarchy. Dermot wanted to create a good spirit within the squad:

'Little things can break the tension for a team. In the strain of an All-Ireland final in 1996 against Mayo Colm Coyle reduced his teammates to laughter when he asked President Mary Robinson, as she was being introduced to the Meath team before the match, with the familiarity of intimacy, "How are things at home?" For the rest of his colleagues the pressure evaporated immediately.

'When I played for Roscommon, especially when we were going well, we always had a great spirit. I think of all the good-natured banter and slagging that went on between the lads. Pat

Lindsay was one of the best players in the country and had massive stature in the dressing-room but I remember Eamonn McManus slagging him off one day about his distribution and telling him that if he ever got up to the half–way line not to try and do anything with it but to give it to someone with a bit of skill on the team.

'There were always some good comments. Tom Heneghan would tell Tom Donlon to take us for a few slow laps around the pitch to start us off. Donlon was very precise and did everything by the book. His idea of slow laps differed radically from that of the players, especially Mick Finneran who was always bringing up the rear. One night as were shuffling into first gear, groaning off the effects of the day before, Finneran was heard to say: "Now Tom. Just slow, just slow." It was a very small remark but it brought giggles of laughter. It broke the tension and got everybody going. So I wanted to have a happy camp when I took over but at the same time one firmly focused on winning.'

It is not necessary to have been a good player, but you do need a particular kind of communication ability to be a manager. The best managers can chart psychological tides. If you don't want problems, don't be a football manager. A manager's effectiveness is largely determined by the way he deals with problems. Every year that a manager is involved with a squad, new problems inevitably arise. It is not possible for 30 people to work together without a few problems. The situation is exacerbated in sport, where competition is intense and emotions are high. Interpersonal problems are inevitable. Such problems must be dealt with as quickly as possible after they appear. Communication is the key to player-manager problems and the lines must be opened as soon as practicable:

'I also wanted all the players to know where we were going as a team but also how they fitted in individually.'

Dermot was a great advocate of the power of attitude: the ability to transmit self-belief to others and to turn that into consistent team success in an increasingly cut-throat business. The great manager in any sport has a rare ability of being able to influence people and alter their attitudes without them being aware that it was happening.

Earley's job was to mould his players with his own defiant spirit and to build a team greater than its sum of its parts. Understanding the complex chemistry of temperaments and moods that is at work in every side he wanted the team to bond around one thing:

'I could never run as fast, or jump as high, or catch as cleanly or kick as straight as when I wore the primrose and blue. I wanted everyone in the squad to share that passion.

'Seamus Hayden tells a story of having a drink with Mick Lyons. A few fans approached them and were shocked by how friendly and easy-going Mick was compared to what he had been on the field. Eventually someone plucked up the courage to say: "Do you know you're a lot different in real life than you were on the football pitch."

Lyons replied: "If the jersey didn't change me, what was the point of wearing it?"

That's the kind of attitude a county player should have.'

Dermot was also determined that his time as a trainer would put the emphasis on skills:

'When Arsene Wenger came to the UK, he stopped all the Arsenal youth teams from playing on full-sized pitches and reduced the number of players, before asking them to play across the pitch instead. That meant that each kid had more touches of the ball at a higher tempo and they improved twice as fast. I wanted my players fit but above all I wanted them to be comfortable on the ball and planned to put that into practice in training.'

Attention to detail was to be another mantra: 'In 1986 Harry Keegan almost single-handedly won a Connacht title for Roscommon with a vintage display. An injury late in the game saw him leaving the pitch and his immediate opponent, Stephen Joyce, took advantage of the situation to score a late winning goal for Galway. The really annoying thing about that game was that Harry had warned the county board that someone would get injured because there was a hole in the pitch but nobody did anything about it. In the end it was Harry himself who ran into it and busted his right ankle. The pain was horrific and Harry had to go off and Stephen won the game for Galway but both the injury and Roscommon's defeat could have been avoided if the right action was taken. I was determined that if any problem like that was identified we would deal with it properly.'

For all his planning there was one factor he would have no control over. Luck. For whom the bell tolls is often a case for whom the ball rolls. Napoleon always wanted lucky generals. He would not have wanted Dermot Earley.

The circle of life

For fans of Gaelic football the Sam Maguire Cup is the Holy Grail. Gaelic Games are one of the few places left where the Corinthian spirit survives where the stars are playing for the love of the game. May is the GAA version of Disneyland. Normal living is magically suspended for a state of communal bliss. It is a license to thrill and be thrilled as each county sets out with a fresh slate hoping that the glory days in September will be theirs. Most fans though are destined for those terrible gut-wrenching days when their team loses. Elation can quickly yield to bitter disappointment. In this corner of the sporting world fans experience more ups and downs than the Emperor Charlemagne. Spectating is no sport for the emotionally unfit. At best it leaves you shattered, at worst it could nearly kill you.

Every year, the annual feast that is the Championship unfolds promising the usual mixture of the complete engagement of the senses, wild abandonment, heart-stopping elation, orgasmic bliss, the sheer toe-curling ecstasy of winning and the adrenalin rush of having the small hairs standing on the back of the neck. Sport is agony and ecstasy. It does not lend itself to grey areas. Many fans though will also experience at first hand the slings and arrows of outrageous fortune and discover just how quickly glory becomes anguish. Fate can be far from kind in the unique roaring crucible of noise that is Croke Park.

As a child growing up in Roscommon football was the battery that drove Dermot's imaginative life and dared him to see Roscommon in a very different light. Football provided an escape from people's problems and anxieties. It allowed them to dream of better days to come. Success, albeit at a very modest level, such as winning the Connacht Championship increased their self-esteem. They walked that little bit taller, they talked just a little more boldly, and they wore their primrose and blue paper caps with pride. When the county team was doing well it didn't seem to hurt as much if the price of cattle was abysmal or if the summer was wet and it was virtually impossible to save the hay or the turf.

Lovely Leitrim

There was to be no quick fix for the Roscommon team and their League form was less spectacular and consistent than he would have liked. Dermot thought deeply in order to discover the right words to explain the course of events in the Connacht Championship in 1993:

'We beat Leitrim in the Connacht semi-final. I knew it would be a difficult match because they were a coming team. People were surprised when they won the Connacht final the following year but I wasn't. John O'Mahony was putting all the blocks in place and they had a real momentum. To add spice to the occasion there was massive rivalry between Leitrim and Roscommon in club football since the infamous "battle of the fog".'

Leitrim champions Aughawillian were playing their Roscommon counterparts Clann na nGael in the Connacht club championship but the match should not have gone ahead. The fog was so bad you could not see the goalie kicking out the ball. Things heated up when two players were hit and soon the whole set of players, subs and supporters were involved. The referee had a hard time getting law and order back but the game was a great battle in every sense.

In 2014, Leitrim's first All-Star winner Mickey Quinn was reminded of the game:
'I met one of the umpires for the first time in almost 25 years. He told me that himself and his fellow umpire were so terrified that they would be assaulted given the atmosphere on the day that they left their white coats beside the goalposts and sneaked out in the fog. There were so many angry fans on the pitch they were terrified they were going to be killed.'

That was one of the reasons why Aughawillian versus Clann was renamed 'the Provos versus the Guards. Leitrim were playing Roscommon in the Connacht Championship in 1990 and before the match their manager at the time P.J. Carroll had an unusual mind game planned. He said: 'Jerome Quinn they all think your f***ing mad in Roscommon, what you need to do is pick up a clump of grass, stick it in your mouth and ate it in front of your marker's face. He'll s**t himself.' Jerome was wing half-back and was marking a lovely, skilful player. Sure enough Jerome did as he was told and you could see the Roscommon player's legs turn to jelly.

Earley went into the semi-final with no more than a tremor of apprehension. When he walked into the dressing-room he could feel the air charged with desire. He knew that his efforts had been rewarded:
'We prepared well for the Leitrim game. They had beaten Galway which caused a bit of a sensation in the media but not to people with an intimate knowledge of Connacht football who saw the way Leitrim were progressing in every game. I was leaving nothing to chance and took them very seriously. Apart from working on our strengths I also looked at their possible weaknesses.

'I told the players before the game that one of their players would be sent off and I told them which one. We had a plan in place to deal with that situation. The game was tight. Sure enough the guy I had predicted was sent off. Our plan kicked in and we closed out the game. I was pleased. The team were buzzing. We were a side on the up. I sensed the mood was exactly right.'

On days like that the worry, the pain, the torment, the thoughtless comments and unexpected traumas and heartache is all worth it because of the buzz, the achievement, the camaraderie and the abiding love of the game itself. Every time you win, it diminishes the fear a little bit more. You can never really cancel the fear of losing; you keep challenging it. Confidence is an intangible and elusive thing, triggered by a proliferation of variable factors from praise from an unexpected quarter to a slight rise in performance levels. When you play well, you never understand how you ever played badly. When you play badly, you never understand how you ever played well. Winning had created the right ambience:

'John O'Mahony talks about taking the opportunity of a lifetime in the lifetime of the opportunity. The Connacht final was our golden opportunity to lay down a marker. I was quietly confident we were going to win and our preparations were good.

'The icing on the cake was that the game was to be played in Hyde Park, which had so many great memories for me, including winning two Connacht finals. This would have been the sweetest of them all. But it was not to be.'

Johnny Giles once said: 'The team with the least ifs, buts and ands always wins the Championship.' There is a lesson for everyone there. Earley learned that lesson very early in his management.

He sat with a studiously impassive face as he tried to make sense of matters 15 years on. He would have needed ice cubes in his blood not to speak without emotion:

'I was really look forward to the game. I felt we could make a breakthrough and announce our arrival on the national stage in Croke Park. I knew we would be in bonus territory after that but a Connacht title would have given us momentum to build into something bigger down the road.

'When I woke that morning my heart sank. It was exactly like the feeling on the morning of the 1980 All-Ireland. The weather was terrible. In fact it was going to be much worse than 1980. I was reminded of growing up in Gorthaganny and the farmers talked of a "slobbery day" and this was going to be one. I could feel the optimism draining out of me but I forced myself to be positive. I had to work hard though to do that because I was determined to project only positive messages to the players.'

He did not want his team to be panicked by the big match atmosphere. There was noise, colour and excitement on each corner. Living through the day was to feel like surfing on an enormous wave: the trick was to stay balanced and to ride the occasion, the danger was to be submerged. He wanted his team playing with intensity but also with control facing the pure physical confrontation so they could harness the power, the speed, the tactics, the courage and the movement - all combing to offer an incomparable, gladiatorial spectacle.

Before the match he delivered his team talk, as if to feed the weakest embers of a fire, with the passion of a man who sincerely believed in his team's ability to win the match. There can be no stronger message for a player on the brink of a major game than an expression of confidence that he has the capacity to win. The importance of the match was clear in every face, a few faces pale with nerves, players who start spitting when they are nervous, were salivating a pool.

Lack of focus

As the hordes of supporters on the pavements and spilling out of the pubs made a dash for the game there was a shocking moment for the Roscommon manager:

'Our County Secretary, Paddy Francis Dwyer, God rest his soul, had purchased a new set of jerseys for the team. The first two jerseys he took out had no numbers on them. For a moment there was panic. What would we do with out numbered jerseys?

Then we discovered the unnumbered jerseys were just spares. Things got back to normal. Shortly afterwards I noticed that one of the players was trying to sneak an unnumbered jersey into his kit bag and that another player was trying to act as a screen for him. I found myself in a dilemma: should I intervene and risk the players going out to play a Connacht final in a state of disharmony or do nothing? I opted for the latter. The loss of two jerseys were insignificant in itself but looking back now it speaks volumes about their focus and commitment less than half-an-hour before playing in a Connacht final.'

As the team emerged from the dressing-room, they were drowned in noise, in unbridled enthusiasm. As they ran on to the field, it felt as if the roar emanated not just from the stands but from every corner of the county. It is hard to explain the depth of emotion throughout a population, isolated and starved for success for so long.

It was to be a case of nothing but the same old story for Earley: 'Again like 1980 it was a game we could have won and should have won. The difference was that this time I had to carry the can. I thought of that match in the last minute of the 1996 All-Ireland final when Colm Coyle kicked the point from way out the field that bounced over the bar. We conceded a freak point like that in '93 and lost the game by a point. On those tiny margins great careers are made or perish.'

Did some of the players let him down that day?

'We lost so it was a case of me letting them down. It was awful weather, an awful game and an awful result. Babs Keating always said there's only 6 inches between a pat on the back and a kick in the arse and I knew if I did not take corrective action there would be severe repercussions for me.'

Typical of Dermot he was able to find a positive note in one of his darkest days like a swaggering little boy, trying to keep his end up after cold water had been poured over his enthusiasm:

'I still remember the horrible empty sensation in the pit of my stomach once the game was over. I wanted to be alone. I wanted to start immediately to put a plan in place to make things right but there were protocols to be observed.

'Although we lost I had to admire the fact that Mayo produced a new star in Kevin O'Neill. I had played against his father, Liam, on many occasions and like his father before him Kevin went on to win an All-Star that year, at just 19 years of age. It was my first time to see him up close and personal and I knew this young man had a special talent.

'That evening a Roscommon fan told me if we had swopped Kevin O'Neill for one of our players not only would we have won the Connacht final but the All-Ireland. It was an exaggeration but it was a fitting compliment to Kevin. Mayo went on to get hammered by Cork in the All-Ireland semi-final. I like to think we would have not capitulated so easily.'

The cynics who predicted that a visit to Croke Park was doomed to failure had all acquired Ph.Ds in, 'I told you so.' Like a log collapsing heavily in the fireplace, sending up a flourish of sparks there would be consequences for the manager:

'The knives were not out for me yet but I knew there would be people sharpening them at the earliest opportunity. That game wasn't my Waterloo but I knew if results did not improve the train would be leaving the station without me on it.'

How did the low compare with losing the All-Ireland final in 1980?

'It wasn't as bad. It was worse. I tried to put on a brave face to the outside world but I knew if we didn't have a good league campaign I would be on borrowed time. We didn't.

'Looking back now that match was the beginning of the tide turning against me as Roscommon manager. The fans hadn't the same confidence in me or the team after that. I hoped it would be a case of needing to take one step back to take two steps forward but that hope was to be misplaced. Our League form was inconsistent and we didn't build the momentum the way I hoped

– but still I still kept faith in the team and the panel. I thought we could give the Connacht Championship a right rattle.'

It is a revealing insight into their League campaign that the most memorable incident came during the winter when he trained the Dublin-based players in the Phoenix Park. One night they were training there a day or two after Earley had substituted a player in a game the previous Sunday. The player in question was unhappy with his substitution. After training the squad normally went to the Aisling Hotel for a meal. However, before joining the others Earley and the player were sitting outside the hotel in the car having a very serious discussion about the player and his future with the team. There was a loud rap on the window. They turned around to see a lady of the night asking them, 'Would you like a good time?'

Last night I had an unpleasant dream

What prompts grown men, not given to weighing the great metaphysical questions, to behave like screaming adolescents? Why do intelligent adults vest their self-esteem in the performance of fifteen young players, mostly in their twenties? Sport is an arena where a society's hopes, ambitions, fears, anxieties and ambivalences have freer play - when arguments about trivialities can escalate into military confrontations. In this way sport serves as a social safety valve and helps integrate a society by providing a soaring saga of a battle against the safe, mundane, killing predictability of everyday life. The oddity in the West of Ireland is that it is an unpredictable, uncertain game like football that has to cope with the feelings of inadequacy and grandiose ambitions of the citizens. There is an incurable optimism which centres around football in western counties. This optimism balances the fatalism and stoicism associated with previous trips to football's theatre of dreams. You do not have to be a heroin addict or a high-wire acrobat to experience extremity. You just have to be a supporter of Connacht football. What the leadership class fail to provide, the county team is expected to do. This was the case before Roscommon faced Leitrim in the 1994 Connacht Championship.

The manager's job, a peculiar mix of amateurism and professionalism, does not deal with or satisfy the need for certitude; it excels in uncertainties and ambiguities Only in matches are the players characters revealed. One has to learn to judge a player or a side on its capacity to cross different and random sets of hurdles and equally on its ability to cross different and random sets of opportunities. One error by a referee can change the complexion of a match altogether. Leitrim kicked their frees. Roscommon did not. Victory has a thousand fathers. Defeat is an orphan.

John O'Mahony was marching to glory and Earley was heading for the exit door.

To neutrals Leitrim's victory was a return to the halcyon days of a moral universe in which the meek could inherit the earth. That sentiment was not shared among Roscommon fans - emitting the sort of body language that would have made the most severe exponents of the Spanish Inquisition seem jovial and tolerant. Misery loves company.

Heroes define a society in more or less the same way as a society defines its heroes. Football fans live with the fantastic and the mythic in a distinctive way. Dermot was to discover that the most strident detractors of the ex-manager and their undisguised antipathy are invariably the same fans who had previously applauded him so lustily.

In conversation with this writer Leitrim's midfield maestro Mickey Quinn observed: 'There were a number of other years where we played Roscommon in the Connacht championship and could have and should have beaten them but that year they should have beaten us. If they scored their frees, our great summer would have ended early.'

His face a study in torture, Dermot refused to accept the obvious excuse for the game. In his regime he was harder on himself than on anyone else: 'Do I blame the free-taker for costing us that match? No. I blame myself.'

Dermot's default position was that the glass was half-full: 'Again I was gutted after the game. This is not an excuse but it was another game that could have gone either way. I think any neutral asked to give an objective analysis would agree that we were in a strong position to win that match. Leitrim proved that they were a very good team, not just by winning the Connacht title but by giving a good game to Dublin in the All-Ireland semi-final.'

No one really believes in the malignancy of gossip, save those who know how they themselves have suffered from it:

'Of course I knew there would be people in the county who had the knives out for me but I still believed in my soul we were a team that could go places. We were close those two years. I felt I could do the necessary fine-tuning to take the team over the line. I still believed in the players and that I was the man to complete the task. Within a few days I was putting plans in place to make some changes for the year ahead but a few weeks later they were taken out of my hands. That was a blow. If I am honest, it was a bad blow.'

There is much romance in Leitrim football though a lot of people keep quiet about it.

Earley could see an aptness in the closure of his Roscommon career: 'I first played for Roscommon in a low key game against Leitrim in 1965 and it was Leitrim who ended my career as Roscommon manager. Looking back now I can see the symmetry in it.'

The brother

Paul Earley played for Roscommon while his brother was manager. It was not the happiest of times for him: 'I had just moved to Sligo. If Dermot hadn't been involved I wouldn't have stayed around because I was having horrific problems with my back. It was not an auspicious time for me or for the team.

'I was looking forward to playing under Dermot but I needed

an hour and a half with my chiropractor before training sessions
and games. The Connacht final in '93 was an awful game. The
weather was awful, with the rain and a gale. We lost by 1-5 to 0-7.
I played badly and the team played badly. It is a game I have tried
hard to forget down the years. I played a few matches in the League
the following season but my back was gone and I had to finish up.
In hindsight, I should have gone much earlier.

'There was one training session I had missed months earlier
because I was physically unable to get into my car. I hadn't rung
Dermot to let him know. He was unhappy with that and had a
conversation with me about it. I should have walked away at that
stage.'

Paul does not go along with the conventional narrative about
the reasons why Dermot's time as Roscommon manager did not
go well: 'I have no time for those who said Dermot was too nice for
the job. That is too simplistic. As always the reasons are more
complex.

'Dermot took over at a time when the county had enjoyed
success but the team was on the way down which is the worst time
to take over a side.

'What may have happened is that Dermot took the job after
being four years in America with the United Nations. He might
have been a little out of touch with the way the game had changed
in the meantime when there had been much greater back-up
structures put in place to assist managers. Under Marty
McDermott, the previous management team had been very
professional and we had won Connacht titles in 1990 and '91.
Dermot was doing everything himself. He was the manager, the
coach, the fitness trainer, the psychologist and so on and would
have been better off delegating some of the workload.

'Early on in his management he was first at training as usual
but the ground was not open. He was very unhappy about that. By
the time the squad arrived the ground was still not open and some
of the players may have felt this did not show the attention to detail

that was required. It wasn't Dermot's fault but some of the players may have not seen it that way.

'I can honestly say I would not be aware of any player who did not give the commitment required but I know that some of those closest to Dermot would feel very strongly that one or two of the best known Roscommon players today from that period let him down badly.

'I never spoke to him about how it finished. I knew he wanted to bring success to the county so badly and he was so disappointed when things did not work out the way he would have wished.'

Amongst Lilywhites

Hope can be like hair - something a lot of men lose as they grow older. Not Dermot Earley. After his stint in charge of Roscommon he was severely deflated. Yet the circle of victory spun incessantly, beckoning him like an irresistible force. Within a few weeks he took over as manager of the Kildare team from Mick O'Dwyer. With his veins coursing with adrenalin, he began to feel an impatient excitement, a need for adventure after weeks off. He was feeling like a boy locked out of Croke Park on All-Ireland final day. History was happening without him.

It is said that courage is not the absence of fear, but rather the judgement that something else is more important than fear. If we turn away from a challenge once, it is so much easier to do the same again the next time, and the next. Showing some courage in less serious difficulties is often the best training for the major crises. Courage is like a muscle. It is strengthened with use. Earley felt it was a time to take his courage in his hands once again. Initially the mood was light. Kildare's problem has always been the lack of scoring forwards:

'Shortly after my appointment I was up on the roof of my two-storey house in Newbridge painting my chimney when a Kildare fan passed by on his bicycle and shouted up at me: "Are you looking for forwards?"

'The first time I managed the team, a Kildare fan came up to me and told me that if I could lead the team to win a Leinster title. Christy Moore would write a song about me. Sadly I got neither a Leinster title nor Christy's song.'

With the benefit of 10 years distance Dermot was philosophical about the way things unfolded with the Kildare team: 'The script for an assessment of my managerial career was written while I was in the Roscommon job. I was determined to put it right and to bounce back straight away but looking back with the benefit of hindsight my own confidence in my ability had been dented a little by the way things finished in Roscommon and I needed time to repair that and also to reflect on what I could learn from that experience.

'I was flattered to be asked to take on the Kildare job. I wouldn't have taken on any other managerial job at the time, except some kind of role in Sarsfields. The fact that I lived in Newbridge and the job was on my doorstep was the deciding factor.'

An initial problem was that he had big shoes to fill when he took the helm: 'Without Kevin Heffernan and Mick O'Dwyer, who knows what Gaelic football management would have been? Micko, the greatest manager of all time, had come into Kildare three or four years earlier and reawakened Kildare as a serious force in football. They were incredibly fit and he re-energised not just the team but the fans and there was a sudden upsurge of interest in the county. There was a buzz I had never experienced in all my years living in Kildare. There were great performances but no trophies and the County Board got rid of him with unseemly haste in the eyes of many.

'When he left it was like a cloud of gloom fell on the fans especially among those who saw him as the Messiah - the only one who could deliver an All-Ireland to Kildare. It was like watching a bicycle getting a puncture and seeing the air drifting out of it.'

In a job in which your reputation is your currency Earley's recent history did not help matters much: 'There was some older fans who saw me as the man who had played so long for Roscommon but there were other who saw me as someone who had failed as a manager in Roscommon. Worse still in the eyes of some my biggest crime was that I wasn't Mick O'Dwyer. The mood music was never right. While ultimately it is about your results the media play a big role in deciding the fate of any new manager. Often they impact on the way some of the players think and that is where they can play a pivotal role.'

When Joe Schmidt first managed Leinster and they lost for the third consecutive time, George Hook said that Schmidt had clearly lost the dressing-room and that he should basically pack it in. The fact that Hook was never in the dressing-room was incidental. The following morning Brian O'Driscoll and Leo Cullen came in together to see him in his office. They told him to completely ignore Hook or any other criticism, that they had 100 per cent faith in what he was trying to do and that all the lads felt the same. They told him not to change anything regarding his approach and that they genuinely believed it would all come together. While the pressure was still on Schmidt had never felt so good. He was still a 'newbie' with the team, but having those two giants of men on his side he knew it would come right. That weekend they played Munster and O'Driscoll scored a late try to win the match, and the team never looked back. Earley would not have such a moment of catharsis.

Dejection

Seasons came and seasons went. Dermot's two year term was not a success: 'The lads tried hard. I tried hard. We had some good performances in the League but we weren't consistent enough. It was frustrating because we had some great players and I knew there was great potential in the squad. These were a group of lads who could go somewhere if we all brought our A-game to the big matches. The cold, harsh reality though is that I won not a single Leinster Championship match with Kildare.'

As things started to unravel his family had to get used to this absorption of his: He would sometimes sit through a meal without speaking, not noticing what he ate, sometimes laying down his knife and fork before his plate was empty, thinking about the problem, his brow heavy with worry: 'When we lost the second year I was in the position no GAA manager wants to be in: standing on the sideline after losing a big match with disappointed players, fans and a county board to be faced, and Marty Morrissey effectively asking me on live television if I was going to consider my position.

'We were beaten and the story could only end one way. Again. Oscar Wilde would have had a field day. To lose one job was bad enough. To lose two in a row in such a short time seemed like carelessness.'

Earley retained one happy memory from his time with Kildare: 'Tradition in Kildare dictated that a representative from the county champions was captain of the team but I broke this tradition and made Glenn Ryan captain. He was only a young man but he rose to the challenge magnificently. When I announced his captaincy there were some raised eyebrows but down through the years as I've watched Glenn become one of the giants of the game, I have a little smile of satisfaction that my judgement in a young player was vindicated.'

The shadow Kildare cast was broadened and darkened by their long years in the wilderness and had the fierce commitment of their people pressing at their backs like a forest fire. It was time for the Lilywhites to rekindle an old friendship: 'In 1964 Joe Lennon published a book called *Coaching Gaelic Football for Champions*. Mick O'Dwyer made a point of not reading it. It didn't seem to do him any harm. The great leader is the one who enthuses others to rally to the cause. He had that gift. Kerry would have won All-Irelands without him because they had so many talented players but they would not have won eight. He kept them wanting to come back for more.

'Micko was brought back and I have to take my hat off to him and give him great credit because he turned the team around and made them one of the best sides in the country, winning two Leinster titles, which was a fantastic achievement.

'How can I put this tactfully? He was very imaginative in his recruitment of players from "outside"! There were some players coming through within the county, like my own son Dermot and the new injection of talent combined with the experience of the older lads made them a force to be reckoned with.'

A semi-detached perspective

In 2001 I spoke to Kildare legend Pat Mangan about those eventful years in the county:

'I did a year as trainer of Kildare myself in 1972-3. Every year we had a different trainer. In fact we had more trainers than Sheik Mohammed! It was a difficult task especially as I found myself doing tasks the County Secretary should have been doing organising matches and pitches etc.

'Mick O'Dwyer brought the organisation and the skill to Kildare football that was lacking over the years. He's a very, very strong personality and the most positive guy that you could ever talk to. A negative would never get into his head. If you were talking to him he'd have you convinced in 10 minutes that you were going to win. He came to Kildare when they were at their lowest. Kildare people love their football and are great supporters but because of that they expect a lot from their team and there's a tremendous tradition of football in the county so that created a lot of pressure and his arrival was headline news so there was a lot of media scrutiny.

'I watched a lot of the trial matches he held at the start and in my opinion Kildare had a very, very ordinary bunch of players. He moulded them together, gave them confidence, and got them exceptionally fit. I would honestly say that in the beginning he got them winning matches against better teams because they were so fit and got them to a League final. Kildare were so fired up by O'Dwyer that they felt they could walk on water. After that he got them to two Leinster finals but when they lost both the hatchet was out again. They literally ran him out of the county.

'Unfortunately Kildare had two bad years after that. In fairness his successor, Dermot Earley, was on a hiding to nothing. Kildare having built up all their expectations found themselves without O'Dwyer. Morale among the players was low and I think Dermot was expected to perform a miracle. They got knocked out in the first round of the championship in consecutive years and the hatchet fell on Dermot. Attendance at club matches were down and Seamus Aldridge and co realised the mistake they had made and brought O'Dwyer back. It was a difficult situation for him. He did an incredible job to lift that team. He had a few good young players coming through and our "imports" were a big help. It's an amazing achievement and I think he was unfortunate not to win an All-Ireland final in 1998 because of all the injuries they had in the run-up though Galway gave a tremendous display on the day.'

The hot seat

In 2013 Roy Keane and Patrick Vieira made a television documentary about their turbulent relationship when they were players. Most of the media comment was, as usual on Keano, but Vieira made some interesting observations about his former boss. The interview unfolded as follows:

Interviewer: 'What is Arsene Wenger's biggest strength?'

Vieira: 'Trust – he believes in players and let's them get on with it.'

'And what is his biggest weakness?'

'Trust. Sometimes players need a kick up the arse.'

It may be that a similar critique could be made of Dermot Earley's managerial career.

The manager serves an interface between the old and the new, the fantastic and the real, the visionary and the practical, the playful and the serious, and the informal and the tactical. Gay Sheeran played under Earley's management. He is ideally placed to evaluate his management style: 'He had a great way about him. There was no roaring or shouting. He was gentle but firm. When he won he never gloated. When he lost he took it on the chin and was always ready to console other players.'

Graeme Souness said: 'I have come to the conclusion that nice men do not make good managers.' Earley believed that sportsmanship does not preclude competition or even aggressive competition, but imposes limits on it, mainly by clearly valuing a sporting defeat more than an unsporting victory: 'It is said that if you are a nice guy you will always be second. I would rather be a nice guy and not a winner, than not be a nice guy and be a winner. But I believe you can be a winner and be nice too. Some people would counter-argue: "Now he is accepting defeat because he is not ruthless." But I was ruthless when I was playing when the ball was near. I did not want to hit anybody out of the way but I would go through him fairly to get the ball! A trainer can get the best out of his players without being ruthless. I favour positive coaching – playing within the rules and working at all times for a raising of standards.'

As a player he saw a role for raising his voice:

'A bit of unexpected verbal aggression can have a positive effect on a player. I remember wining a ball against Offaly, in the League semi-final in 1979, under Hill 16 and seeing the field open up in front of me. I passed the ball to Eamonn McManus who was just in front of me and shouted at him "to get up the f***king field". He took off like a rocket. He told me afterwards that he was scared out of his wits.

'When Dublin faced Meath after their 1983 All-Ireland victory Gerry McEntee said in the Meath dressing-room: "Let's clap them on to the field. We have to do that and then let's kick the living shite out of them." There is a place in the game for that kind of dogged determination.'

When all is said and done

Despite the protestations of Joe Brolly Gaelic games are now a result business. Many managers made the same discovery as Graeme Souness after he was sacked as Liverpool manager, which he blamed on the persisitent hostility of much of the media against him. As Ronnie Whelan, himself a casualty of Souness at Anfield when he was sold permaturely, incisively observed: 'Souness is complaining the papers had him sacked. They did. They printed his results.'

The general view, sometimes reiterated like a magic spell, was that Earley failed on the sideline. In an uncharacteristically grim face, as though carved from folded granite he appraised his own record as manager:

'In June 1989 the late Seán Doherty sensationally lost his seat in Roscommon in the General Election. On live television as he stood in the Roscommon count centre Brian Farrell asked him: "Seán Doherty, what went wrong?"

With a typical smile he replied: "Not enough people voted for me, Brian."

'The reality is I didn't win a Connacht title with Roscommon or a Leinster title with Kildare or even a Railway Cup with Connacht. In the light of those stark facts I have to conclude that my career as a manager was a failure.'

As a race we are always happy to blame somebody else. Flann O'Brien claimed that he wrote *At Swim-Two-Birds* in order to become a millionaire; and he liked to complain that Hitler started a war a few weeks after publication just to frustrate this noble enterprise. Earley was not in that category: 'I was greatly honoured to get each of these jobs but I didn't deliver the results I hoped to achieve. I have no excuses. The buck stops with me.'

The role of a sports coach is to ensure that the footballer is prepared to meet a challenge and come through it as a winner. Often the mental preparation is as important as the physical. Winning in sport requires striking the correct balance between desire to win and fear of failure. It is relatively easy to let the fear of failure get the upper hand and to shrink into passivity and thinking. Players must not only want to win enough, but they must believe that they can win, and be prepared to persist until they do. Of all the variables the most fragile element is belief in their ability to win. A belief in their ability to turn a situation around has seen a team like Meath through many a crisis:

'I went in each of my managerial jobs hoping and expecting to create a culture of winning. I failed to do that and my teams failed as a result. I, and I alone, have to take the blame for that.'

The role of the inter-county manager has become part of the entertainment industry – as a new item of mass consumption. Gaelic football involves playing dice with destiny. It has ways of subverting the best-laid plans:

'Gaelic football offers an enormous number of excuses for failure, the absence of the killer instinct, an off-day for the free taker, the referee, the umpires, the weather. For many fans though the issue is much simpler: it's the manager's fault. In that perspective the solution is very simple: sack the manager. I understand that's the way the game is played and that is why I had to walk the plank.'

I put it to Dermot that there was a perception within Roscommon that some players on the team had not given him the commitment he required. I repeated a conversation with a mutual friend who had named a few specific players who he claimed "rode" Dermot for the two years. He paused for a long time before answering. It was clear that he was walking a tightrope between answering the question as honestly as possible and being diplomatic:

'I would say a few things about that. First, there were many players in the squad who gave everything I could have asked and some even more than I could have reasonably expected.

'Secondly, I'm not going to disparage on players on that team. Each of us when we look at ourselves honestly in the mirror is responsible for own attitude and our own actions. It is not for me to sit in judgement. Ultimately each of us is responsible for what we did and what we failed to do. I don't judge those who try and fail but only those who fail to try.

'The longer I live, the more I realise the impact of attitude on life. We cannot change our past. We cannot change the inevitable. The only thing we can do is play on the one string we have - namely our attitude. I am sympathetic to the view that life is 10 per cent what happens to you and 90 per cent how you react to it.'

The psychological scars of those four years did linger:

'One of my first lessons in my army training was that whoever wins the war writes the history regardless of what the facts were. As a player from the moment I first pulled on the shirt for the Roscommon minors I was never perceived as a failure – but now people were talking openly about me being a failure as a manager.

'Let's make no bones about it none of us are immune from the way others see us. It does hurt when people do not think well of you and it does cause you, in your dark moments, to question yourself. I know people use the example of soccer and say managers are sacked every day but they are paid off handsomely to walk away so we are talking about apples and oranges.'

From the time he became manager Dermot felt as if he was living a life of perpetual surprises – one foot in compulsory illusion and the other in secret reality:

'Would I do things differently if I got the chance? Yes. If I knew then what I knew now would I have taken those jobs? One side of my brain says I would be mad to. But the romantic, if that's the right term, in me would still be tempted. Football is the one area where my heart too often ruled my head. Do I regret that? Yes and no. I could never regret working with players and trying to improve them, even when the results were disappointing. But sometimes I look back and think of the cost to my family.'

The one consolation was that he gave it a go:

'Things did not go the way I would have liked in Roscommon

or Kildare but at least I will not die wondering what would have happened if I took either job.'

On a lighter note if a fairy godmother granted him one wish for his time as manager what would it be?

'A football career, like a life, is measured in moments rather than in days. One vignette that typifies Offaly's Matt Connor's career came for his club Walsh Island (whom he steered to six consecutive county titles between 1978 to 1983) in Newbridge, in a Leinster club match. His side was under pressure and needed a score. Matt collected the ball 25 yards out from his own goal and went the length of the field on a solo run. In his green and white hooped jersey he left everybody that came to tackle him behind, stretched on the ground, without any of them even touching him, where he swerved, feinted, sold a dummy, slowed up or accelerated to lose his man. As the ball went over the bar some of the players he had beaten were still on the ground, some were picking themselves up and one or two were on one knee. All were pictures of dejection, beaten by superior skills. So if I had a wish for my time in either Kildare or Roscommon it would be to have had a forward of the same class as Matt.'

While he did not have the managerial career he would have wished for as a player Earley left an indelible mark on the football landscape.

3

Primrose and Blue

FOR many of us, sport kindles memories of triumphs and tragedies in childhood, adolescence and adulthood; it cloaks a field of dreams. There is an exquisite self-contained quality about an All-Ireland final. All the build-up matches, whatever their own resplendent excitements, can only nourish the expectations of that ultimate collision. All irrelevance is cast aside. The semi-finals offer sudden death but this is the only one that tantalisingly offers instant immortality. No matter how many teams have started out, regardless of backdoors or side doors, in the final only two can play, and only one can win.

Those whose childhood and adolescence was thrilled by Micheal O'Hehir have been permanently impregnated with the mythology of Gaelic games. The All-Ireland final is more than a mere sporting contest, it is inevitably a spiritual and identity-forming occasion. In that heightened sense of anticipation even the most trivial preliminary is invested with a tremor of pleasure. Bad jokes seem funny. Complete strangers take on friendly faces. Supporters are even more raucously lively and colourful than usual. Opposing fans, with sometimes gigantic flags streaming behind tall poles thrust from their car windows, weave hazardously to Drumcondra, seeking victims for their banter. Predictions and extravagant statements abound with little place for objectivity.

Croke Park on All-Ireland final day is sacramental, a transcendental experience that calls automatically upon systems of thinking and feeling with a whole undergrowth of behaviour and sentiment and attitude. It satisfies so much in GAA folk that pines consciously or unconsciously for appeasement: a worthy stop-off on an unfinished and unfinishable journey for heroic feats rendered into the ever-stable currency of sporting legend. Dermot Earley though was not to savour the sweetest prize for any player in the GAA's theatre of dreams. Nonetheless it is better to win glorious triumphs, even if checkered with failure, than to inhabit the grey twilight that knows not victory nor defeat.

After his death it almost became a cliché to say he was 'the greatest player never to have won an All-Ireland.' Jimmy Magee though is keen to pay tribute in more positive terms:

'Dermot was kinda part of my life. He wasn't a close friend but he was a friend. He always seemed as if he was happy to see you and I am sure he was. He had an endearing smile and a great personal warmth.

'Men are not judged in my lifetime by the number of honours but by their behaviour in the pursuit of honours. He had the greatest medal of all. He had respect. Wouldn't that be great to have on your tombstone? "This man had great respect".'

That same respect was again in evidence as Tony Hanahoe imagined Kevin Heffernan picking the 'team of the Heavens' at Heffo's funeral in 2013:

'I'll have Lar Foley, Paddy Bawn Brosnan, Enda Colleran, Páidí O'Sé, Tim Kennelly . . . they're the backs. Des Foley, John Timmons, Purcell, Freaney . . . Dermot Earley, Frankie Stockwell . . . I'll build around the rest.'

Regrets I have a few

For Dermot Earley the fascination with Gaelic games arrived like talking, too early to remember. The disappointment of not winning an All-Ireland was as nothing compared with his misery at his failure to live up to his own standards. High fliers can singe their wings. His regret, that causes a preoccupied pause in the midst of uttering a sentence, is palpable. The first such lapse was his blackest day in the primrose and blue.

In 1975 Roscommon played in a league match. In the course of the game Earley was fouled and fell heavily as the sizable frame of Jimmy Keaveney came tumbling down on top of him. As Earley rose to his feet a scuffle broke out in which there were four minor altercations with Dublin's Bobby Doyle. After the fourth incident Earley's patience snapped and he punched Doyle on the nose. Nothing electrifies the crowd like a good fight and there was kind of surging forward and backward and growing thicker and thicker as people got the news that finally, thank God, something interesting was about to happen. The referee had no option but to send him off. As he made the lonely journey to the dug-out Earley's brain was spinning and his spirits were absolutely crushed:

'It was the most devastating thing that ever happened to me playing football – much worse than losing the All-Ireland. As I walked back to the line the realisation of all the things that were going to happen came.

'I always tried to be as fair as I could. Even if I fouled I always felt it was wrong afterwards. I would be concerned if I fouled in the course of the game on a number of occasions. To be warned by a referee is a blot on your copybook but to be sent off is incredible.'

Although he was just a young boy at the time Paul Earley remembers that day well:

'I have to confess I remember being delighted he did what he did that day. I always felt that he took much punishment on the pitch without taking any action. When the game was over our eyes met through the crowd. He came over to me with his head down in a state of total dejection. He was unable to look me in the eye as he said: "I'm sorry I let you down".'

The sending off was extensively reported the next day in the newspapers. The incident was the major talking point as his colleagues gathered for their coffee break in the morning. When Earley walked in to the officer's mess there was a sudden silence:

'Someone asked me if I had anything to say and I replied: "I shouldn't have done it." After that everything went back to normal.'

The situation was complicated by the fact that Earley was due to travel with the All-Stars the following month to America. The rule at the time was that any player who was sent off was ineligible to be selected for the All-Stars that year. Would Earley make the touring party?

The situation was resolved shortly after when he received a telegram from the legendary John Kerry O'Donnell in New York who offered to pay his expenses for the trip because:

Red-blooded men are welcome in Gaelic Park.

Although he did travel Earley regretted it. He had been given to understand that he would be part of the touring side, the same as everybody else but that was not the case. This was brought home to him almost immediately. A welcoming committee greeted the team at the airport. Each player was called forward individually and presented with an envelope which included details of accommodation, itinerary and the allowance provided for the tour. Although Earley was called forward there was no envelope to be found for him. He wished the ground would open and swallow him he was so embarrassed. Similar incidents were to occur three more times on the tour.

However, the most galling part came at the end of the tour when a non-GAA travelling official reminded him that John Kerry O'Donnell had paid his expenses on the tour and accordingly he should thank John Kerry before he left. Earley felt like the most junior pupil in school receiving a lecture from the headmaster. Such a reminder was totally unnecessary.

Not a Longford Leader

The second sour memory for Dermot was in a match against Longford when Roscommon were badly beaten and he had the proverbial stinker:

'I played absolute rubbish. When the full-time whistle went I was absolutely disgusted with my performance and annoyed that Longford beat us so easily. I was marking Seán Mulvihill, Liam's brother, and he had not allowed me a touch of the ball in the whole game. He was a player I knew very well, having spent a year with him studying P.E. in Strawberry Hill in London and we won the All-Ireland seven-a-side together. I would have considered him a good friend. He held out his hand for me to shake but I was so sick with my inability to play well that in frustration I walked away without shaking hands. I am still haunted by that memory.'

As the rain slid along the windows giving a false sense of early evening his voice became detached and clinical because of a third painful memory - a League match against Kerry in Tralee, playing full-forward on John O'Keeffe. Earley was unable to cope with the mastery of his opponent. In the final moments in a gesture of pure frustration Earley struck him a blow in the stomach. There was little force in the blow but the aggression was out of character:

'As soon as I hit him I regretted doing it. John's reaction was that of a gentleman. When the full-time whistle blew I apologised to him and I can remember him saying: "I know that's not like you." Somehow this made me feel much worse. It was something that I regretted very much.'

He ain't heavy. He's my brother

Closer to home there was another painful memory. The Secret Footballer (a mystery star player who writes an acclaimed column in an English newspaper under the cloak of anonymity) has become compulsive reading for his series of perceptive insights into the world of English football, and in 2012 his book was voted sports book of the year. He describes going to see his young son play his first schoolboy match. Just before kick-off he had this urge to shout soomething inpsirational to his flesh and blood. He roared: 'JUST DON'T BE SH*T, OK?' To his mortification Dermot did something worse as he recalled with the anguish in his voice raising with each sentence. Still waters run deep:

'My brother Paul (who is seventeen years younger than Dermot) was playing in his first final in Castlerea. My father had told me the game was going on and I made a special effort to attend. Paul's team were not doing well, the other team were much stronger. I had expected a lot from Paul because of the stories I had heard about him. In that situation I felt that they needed something special. When the half-time whistle came Daddy asked me to go in and say a few words. I told Paul that he needed to make a major effort in the second-half. I was critical of him for not being more mobile on the field. When he got the ball he was very skilful and made some great passes and got some great points from frees. I gave out to him. I told him he was lazy. This was not the way to approach an eight-year-old. He was very shocked that I had spoken like this. I know it was the wrong thing to do and I have regretted it many times since.'

The Young Ones

Gaelic games, even though they may be occasionally disfigured by the intrusion of cheap and distorted values, still offers a context in which the really big spirit can express itself. As a young player Earley did have the advantage of being in at the start of the great television adventure, when the black-and-white grainy pictures of live football were a wondrous excitement for a generation whose years had been spent grasping mind pictures from the words of radio commentators.

In 1965 he made his senior intercounty debut in a real prestigious fixture: a Gael Linn game against Leitrim. Surprisingly his first game in this unglamorous outpost of football was as a right half-back.

History bestowed upon him a unique distinction he cared nothing about. He was the first player in history to play inter-county football at minor, under-21, junior, and senior levels in the one year. Tyrone's Frank McGuigan was the second.

1966 would see Earley win an All-Ireland under-21 medal. For an independent perspective on the game I spoke with Kildare stalwart Pat Mangan: 'We were red hot favourites to retain our title.

We had twelve of the team that had won the previous year. We waltzed through Leinster without being put under any pressure. We beat a very good Kerry team well in Newbridge to win the semi-final and I'd say we were unbackable favourites to win the final. Roscommon didn't have an impressive semi-final performance and the scribes and obviously a lot of Kildare players thought it was going to be one-way traffic. The dedication and commitment was lacking and we got caught on the hop. In a number of matches in the campaign we had struggled for long periods of the games but then once we turned it on we blew the opposition out of the water.

'In the second half of the All-Ireland we stepped up a gear and moved about five points clear of Roscommon and looked to be coasting home. If there was an incident which turned the match I think it was when our centre half-back, Pat Nally, went off with a groin injury he had carried into the game. I was moved back to centre-back and Roscommon who had been struggling moved Dermot Earley to midfield. He pumped in a few great balls to the forwards and Roscommon got two goals from them. Roscommon went a point up with about a minute to go. Kildare got the ball from the kick out and I remember Pat Dunny cutting in from the left hand side and he was between the 21 and the 14. He thought we were two points down and went for a goal but his shot was blocked down. I've no doubt if he knew the score he would have taken the point and the game would have been a draw and we would have won the replay.'

Galway boy's hurrah

All teams in Connacht at the time were very much in the shadow of Galway's three-in-a-row (1964-6) All-Ireland winning side. Earley was a big admirer of that team and they helped shape his own philosophy of Gaelic football:

'They had great players individually but were also a great unit. Likewise Mick O'Dwyer's Kerry were a team with all the roles. The teams that are most successful are the teams that mould as a team.

If a team has one or two great players you can always blot them out and you can take them but you can't blot out six class forwards. You couldn't single out any one player on that Galway side. They were a team of stars.'

Earley quickly was to find himself in the company of the stars of that side when he quickly graduated to the Connacht team. He learned a lot about proper preparation from those players:

'Sometimes the little things can reveal a lot. I once asked the great Galway goalkeeper Johnny Geraghty when he first knew that the three-in-a-row Galway side of the sixties was on the way down. He replied immediately, "The first time somebody came into training without their boots clean."'

He also learned how spiteful the fans can be from another Galway legend:

'Jack Mahon once bumped into a young fella in Galway and was a bit disappointed to hear that the youngster had never heard of him. He hoped he might impress his new acquaintance when he told him that he played at centre half-back on the Galway team that beat Cork in 1956.

"Gosh that's shocking", said the youngster.

"Why?", asked a bemused Jack.

"Because I've just discovered my Dad's a liar. He's always said that when Galway won that All-Ireland they never had a centre-back!"'

The talent pool grows

Initially there was a great burden on Earley's shoulders as some of the fans expected him to carry the team on his own:

'When people talk about the giants of Roscommon football they talk about Jimmy Murray and Gerry O'Malley and rightly so. But take it from someone who knows because I played with him for so long up there at the top and I mean the very, very top is Harry Keegan. For any Roscommon player to win three All-Stars is an incredible achievement.'

That same year another talent emerged with a heart as big as a cathedral and the skill to go with it:

'To add to our great good fortune we discovered another great full-back in Pat Lindsay at exactly the same time. If someone ever asked me to define reliability I would need just two words: Pat Lindsay.

'Mick Freyne was a serious forward and in 1972 became Roscommon's first All-Star winner. In 1972 I felt we were going places.'

His confidence was almost put to the sword before the summer had begun. In all of Harry Keegan's performances for Roscommon he played with the intensity of a medieval martyr. Despite his toughness he only got one booking in his playing days.

Yet his career almost perished before it begun:

'If I remember rightly Harry first played for Roscommon in a League match in 1972 against Kilkenny. A few months later we played Galway in the Connacht semi-final in Roscommon. We were leading by 12 points at half-time and the perception was that the referee gave everything to Galway. John Tobin kicked frees for fun and the match ended in a draw. The crowd were incensed and broke through the fences to attack the referee. It was a real mob scene. John Morley was on duty that day and stood in front of the referee and only for that he might have been killed or certainly very badly injured. The ref was struck though and Harry and another player, Martin Silke were accused of hitting him. In fact the ref was hit but by another Roscommon sub. They were both brought up before the Connacht Council. It was very serious for Martin as he was a garda and if he had been found guilty of assault it would have major repercussions for his career. Likewise Harry had just begun his nursing career in St Ita's Portrane and if a finding of assault was upheld against him it would have been very damaging professionally.

'The maddening thing for Harry was that when the incident happened he was 30 yards away. Harry had been marking Seamus

Leydon that day and Seamus wrote a letter to the Connacht Council. I have heard a lot of talk about sportsmanship throughout my career but I always thought that was such a brilliant sporting gesture. The night of the inquiry the legendary Seán Purcell spoke on Harry's behalf as well. The frustrating thing was neither the referee nor the umpires turned up. They were put through all that stress for nothing.

'We beat Galway in the replay in the Tuam. Tom Heneghan was put on John Tobin that day and Tobin didn't get a smell of the ball. Tom was just the man to "put manners" on a player like Tobin.'

Fortified by rosy speculation about how his men might march majestically to glory Castlebar would bring a breakthrough:

'We beat Mayo in the Connacht final with a very young side. Our oldest player was Jimmy Finnegan who was 26. We were badly beaten by Kerry in the All-Ireland semi-final. The big disappointment was not that we lost but that we didn't play as well as we could. The same thing happened against Kerry in the semi-final in 1978. Losing but playing well may not be much of a consolation but it is a crumb of comfort. When you get to Croke Park and play one of the top teams you want to play to your best and it hurts when you fail to do so. We always looked forward to playing Kerry. They are the aristocrats of football. They are the yardstick to measure how good you are, personally and as a team.'

That 72 semi-final was to prove memorable for Harry Keegan for all the wrong reasons: 'Harry got his right ankle injured that day and the injury was to persecute him for the rest of his career. He had to go off and that was the sort of blow we could have done without. We trained very hard for that game but left our fitness on the training ground. We were really flying two weeks after. The game is probably most remembered for the long time Mick O'Connell sat down in the middle of the pitch tying his laces. To some people in Roscommon it was a bit disrespectful.'

Two years later Kerry were to ruin Roscommon's hopes again:

'We completely outplayed them in every sector of the field in the National League final but John Egan got a last minute goal to equalise the game. They beat us easily in the replay. To beat Kerry in a national final in Croke Park would have been a huge boost to that team and set us up for greater things. Instead we were again badly beaten in the Connacht final by a very strong Galway side who were unlucky not to have won an All-Ireland final in the early 1970s.'

Glory Days

1977 saw the beginning of the most glorious phase in Earley's career as Roscommon won the first of four consecutive Connacht titles:

'I had missed two years on peacekeeping duties abroad but when I came back the team was definitely stronger because we had picked up some great talent. Roscommon Gaels were motoring well and qualified for an All-Ireland final and John O'Gara burst on the scene from that side. Eamonn McManus had arrived and made a great contribution over many years.'

As a celebrator and evangelist of Gaelic football's capacity to enthrall and entertain, Earley sought out original talent and the spark of creativity where he could see the light of new hope and aspiration beginning to spark in the eyes of the players he was playing with. Roscommon's first game in the Championship was against Mayo in Castlebar. The home side were first out of the traps and build up a lead but for Earley the changing fortunes were encapsulated in one incident. In the few seconds that followed a torrent of thoughts rushed through his mind:

'Mick Finneran first announced himself to us in the Connacht championship in 1977 when he came on as a sub against Mayo, having played earlier in the minor match. Just as I was placing the ball for a long distance free this young whippersnapper came running beside me and whispered to me: "Give the ball to me and I will give it back to you." I did as I was ordered, taking a quick free to Mick, and got the ball back much closer to the goal and slotted it over the bar. I knew then we would win the game comfortably.

'Although he had incredible skill and the best sidestep and dummy I ever saw Mick was not known for his work rate. Another very clear memory I have of him is against Down in Newry in a challenge match. We put him as a raw 18-year-old in at full-forward on the Down and Ulster full-back at the time. Mick gave him the mother and father of all roastings and scored six points in the first half. All he needed was a yard and the ball was over the bar.

'He got RTE's goal of the season in 1979 in the All-Ireland semi-final against Dublin. The great pity for Roscommon football was that he gave it up so quickly because he was an outstanding talent and if you matched his flair with a fraction of Harry Keegan's dedication you would have had one of the all time greats.'

Three Leaf Shamrock

Any joy Earley experienced in Roscommon's Connacht semi-final victory over Sligo was offset by the tragic events of 19 June, 1977: 'Three young men were returning home to my own village of Gorthaganny, on the Roscommon-Mayo border, having attended a Connacht semi-final between Roscommon and Sligo, when their car was crushed by a train at a railway crossing. To this day the cause of the crash has not been clearly established.

'Today a tombstone in the shape of a shamrock in the graveyard in Gorthaganny provides a permanent reminder of the tragedy. In the leaves of the shamrock are photographs of the three victims Tom Flanagan, Joe Gorman and Michael Mahon. I was a friend and neighbour to the three men who lost their lives.'

A dramatic one point Connacht final victory was secured with a late goal in the Hyde despite a stellar performance from Galway's Brian Talty and Earley having the middle finger of his right hand severed in an accidental clash with Johnny Hughes. He was left with an enduring legacy from the game with a line across his middle finger with five little strokes which mark the points of his five stiches.

Controversy

Earley found himself embroiled in controversy in the All-Ireland semi-final against Armagh. With the score tied at Armagh 3-9 Roscommon 2-12 as Earley faced up to a long distance free, the last kick of the game, Gerry O'Neill (brother of Irish manager, Martin), the Armagh trainer, ran across the field in front of him and shouted something at him. The kick sailed high and wide. There was much press comment on the 'O'Neill-Earley' incident in the following days. In his column in *The Evening Press* Con Houlihan offered two All-Ireland tickets to the person who could tell him what O'Neill said to Earley. The Roscommon star was not unduly distracted: 'I had no idea what he said to me that time. I wasn't even aware that he was talking to me. All I wanted to do was drill the ball over the bar.'

What did bother him was the outcome of the game:

'We were seven points up with 10 minutes to go in the All-Ireland semi-final against Armagh but we lost concentration and let them back to draw the game. You could feel the giddiness running through the team. We thought we had one foot in the All-Ireland final. We were shell-shocked in the dressing-room afterwards. We had been much better than them but in the replay they beat us by a point.

'It was pretty much the same story two years later when we snatched defeat from the jaws of victory against Dublin in the semi-final to again lose by a point. If we had won either of those two semi-finals the experience of having played an All-Ireland final would have been invaluable when we took on Kerry in the 1980 final.'

It is not the loss in the replay in 1977 that most irks Harry Keegan today:

'Everybody keeps talking about the Kerry-Dublin semi-final that year and it's regularly shown on tv but people forget that we produced two great entertaining games, which almost 100,000 people came to watch. Yet neither of the games is ever shown on television. The other so-called "classic" was really a game of rugby league, there was so much hand-passing. We played Armagh again in the 1980 semi-final and that was a very entertaining, high-scoring game but it is never shown on tv whereas our final in 1980 is shown, even though it is a much poorer game.'

Clashes between Armagh and Roscommon would continue to provide many memorable moments down the years. In 1982 they met for a series of three matches in America. Before the first match some of the players had partied too hard and went onto the pitch in something less than the full of their health. At one point the ball was coming in towards the Armagh goal. Their accomplished full-back Jim Kerr went for the ball but was experiencing a form of double vision and he went up for the ball but caught an imaginary ball, toe-tapped it and cleared it. Meanwhile a Roscommon player had caught the real ball and stuck it in the net. When interrogated about the mishap Kerr's response contained no admission of guilt, 'I got the ball I went for!'

Harry Keegan has one particularly strong memory of playing Armagh: 'We played them in a fierce match in the League at the height of the Troubles. There was a skirmish and a lot of "scelping" in that match. They beat us by a point. We were delighted they beat us because there were rocks and stones reigning down on us after the game in the dressing-room. What would they have done if we won! It was not one of my favourite places to go as they were one of the few crowds I found abusive. I'm sure the Troubles did have an impact on them but I couldn't understand why they took it out on Roscommon above any team.'

We're going to America

The upturn in Roscommon's fortunes would see Earley heading across the Atlantic Ocean: 'Long before Cork made striking fashionable in the GAA we were the first to threaten to use player power. We were in New York to play Kerry in the Cardinal Cushing

Games over two matches. We beat them initially in a thirteen-a-side in the first game. We had been promised money from John Kerry O'Donnell, who was "Mr. GAA" in New York. We knew for a fact that Kerry had been paid but we got nothing and we were running short of money. We held a council of war. As I was the army man it was appropriate that I chaired it! The word was sent back to John Kerry – no money no playing. As far as I know we were the first county to threaten to strike!

'Another memory I have of the trip is that we were invited to a formal reception hosted by the Lord Mayor. It was a real big deal for the County Board. The problem was that the heat was almost unbearable. One of the lads brought down a keg of beer to keep himself distracted from the heat! Gerry Beirne went so far as to take off his shirt which was a major breach of protocol. The message quickly came down from the top table from the county chairman, Michael O'Callaghan, to get it back on quickly.'

The American influence was soon felt in an unexpected way in Roscommon when team coach Seán Young asked the players to kneel down and say a prayer before running out on the pitch: 'That kind of thing is big in American football. That said when a manager spends ten minutes trying to whip you up into a frenzy it is a very dramatic change of tone to be told to kneel down and say a *Hail Mary*. Is that the best way to prepare for a big match? I'm not convinced.'

Earley was very appreciative of the role played by the Roscommon County Board throughout his playing career though their methods were unorthodox:

'They always looked after us even if the money wasn't too generous. One incident stands out for me. After a Connacht final in the '70s Harry Keegan went to one of the top officials in the County Board and told him that he needed money for expenses. He brought Harry out to his car, opened the boot and pulled out a £100 note from a green wellington and handed it to him. He then told Harry to send in the docket for it.

'It was very much a give and take situation. They were good to us and we were good to them. To take one example they looked after Tony McManus very well when he was in College, giving him extra expenses than normal when he needed them and while he was in College, Tony went on two All-Star trips as a replacement and got extra cash to help him. That was very fair and he treated them very fairly afterwards. Tony never put in for expenses in his latter years with Roscommon.'

There was one time when the county board did, albeit unwittingly, make the players job a little harder: 'We played Armagh in the All-Ireland semi-final. We had worn our alternative colours, a blue jersey with a gold hoop, something like the Tipperary colurs but they were immensely heavy, far heavier than any jersey I had ever worn before. It was a very hot day and they were not very suitable. When I gave my jersey to Jimmy Smyth, he said in his best Armagh accent: "God ye were wearing bloody anoraks out there today".'

Hey Mr. Postman

One of the healthier legacies of the education system bequeathed by the many religious orders in Ireland was the inclusion of the value of service alongside personal development, emotional satisfaction, monetary reward and occupational status, as the goals of education. This nurtured notions of communal purpose and social value prompted many people to dedicate so much of their lives as volunteers for the GAA.

At the time Roscommon had such a figure on the sideline: 'One of the great characters of Roscommon football was Danny Burke, a team selector and a postman in Castlerea. Before one of our Connacht finals the announcer called out Danny's name instead of our star half-back Danny Murray. It got the biggest cheer of the day.

'At that stage if we went down injured, Danny was the man who looked after you. Danny had absolutely no medical knowledge. Now, things are a lot more sophisticated with proper medical back-up. We will never forget the day Eamonn McManus got a kick in the groin and Danny was in like a flash. After examining Eamonn carefully he said, "One, two, you're alright, they're still there"!' Danny Burke was an integral part of the team rituals and they can mean a lot. One of the small rituals Joe Schmidt brought to the Leinster rugby team from his Clermont days was shaking hands when you meet someone for the first time that day. It was something the players really took to. Jamie Heaslip in particular is a big fan, and would go out of his way to shake hands with the young academy lads he sees, which gives them a huge lift. When Schmidt himself chatted to these young lads they would all say that a Jamie handshake really gave them a great boost and gave them such a strong feeling of belonging to the group – an illustration of one of Dermot Earley's dogmas that little things can have a big impact.

Revenge is sweet

The glory of a second consecutive Connacht final victory in 1978 was quickly dissipated by a crushing defeat to Kerry in the All-Ireland semi-final. Revenge though came quicker than might have been expected with of the great days in Roscommon history: 'Roscommon beat Kerry in the under-21 All-Ireland final. Kerry were very cocky and allowed us to play the match in Roscommon. I know it still rankles with some Kerry people that they conceded home advantage to us and made our task a lot easier. In the warm-up match we had a rare victory over Kerry in the Ceannarus tournament in the senior team so it was a very sweet memory for us all and for the fans.

'Long term the consequences for the senior team were significant. Roscommon picked up some really class players from that under-21 side the likes of Seamus Hayden, Gerry Connellan and, of course, Tony McManus.'

Many Western counties have fallen short in Croke Park for lack of a top class forward. That team supplied Roscommon with one of the best. Off the field Tony McManus moves with unaffected grace. Despite a sense of habitual calm, which is communicated by the soft voice in which he speaks his well-constructed sentences, and the expression of amiable serenity that is usually on his face on the field he was as incisive and as deadly as a meat cleaver. His absolute awareness of where the danger and opportunity lie at any moment enabled him to materialise in front of goal with interventions that were as final as death.

For Tony McManus the appreciation was reciprocated: 'It was great to be a corner forward with Dermot Earley at midfield. He hit a tremendous long ball to you on your outside, giving you the chance to win the ball.'

For many people 1979 is remembered as the year the pope came to Ireland. For Earley the abiding memories were of a first ever defeat of Kerry in the National League quarter-final. An emphatic defeat of Cork in the League final would give Earley his only senior national honour:

'I was surprised we beat Cork so easily in that League final. Cork had a team of stars, including Jimmy Barry-Murphy who was lethal from 12 yards but Tom Heneghan had him in his pocket that day.'

Earley's majestic fielding was a feature of the game. A banner in the stand had been prophetic: 'Earley to rise.' Although a long night of revelry lay ahead there was one disappointment for him in the game:

'Despite his long service to the county Harry Keegan missed out on our only national title in that era. Although his replacement Seamus Tighe had a fantastic game, Harry was a mere bystander because of a hamstring injury. Hamstrings were the bane of his life. During training he would have to hold himself back to try and protect them but by God he gave it all in the games. He really had to mind himself and there was no drinking, especially because he was living and working in Dublin and he had a lot of travel to deal with. Harry didn't tog out that day which I think was a mistake because he wasn't seen to be part of the squad the same as the rest of us. The only time the Roscommon team went up the steps of the Hogan stand to collect a cup Harry was in the stand.'

The League title was a glowing endorsement of Tom Heneghan's managerial career, displaying an impressive knack of extracting the maximum from the abilities at disposal, of claiming more than the going rate for their skills. Roscommon would again advance through Connacht but only after coming through a stiff challenge against Mayo in the Connacht final. There was a particular enjoyment for Earley in that occasion: 'I was thrilled because my good friend through the army Seán Kilbride turned in an inspirational performance in the second half which turned the tide in our favour. Seán had played so well for so many years for Mayo but had transferred to us and his value to us was really shown in that game.'

Next up, in a ground that can be the most exhilarating or the most intimidating in Gaelic games, was a game with bountiful echoes of past dramas for Roscommon. At the end the supporters could find nothing to praise but the weather: 'We lost the All-Ireland semi-final to Dublin later that year. It was our third year in a row to lose a semi-final and that does play on your mind. You wonder if you will ever make it. We only lost by a point but it was a case of so near yet so far. We didn't have the killer instinct to put them away when the game was ours for the taking. Some of the lads always felt that in those sort of games the referee gave the benefit of the doubt to the "big counties" like Dublin.'

Pat Spillane tan

Earley had a distraction before the Championship began in the new year. He had been invited by RTE to compete in their Sports Superstars Championship to be recorded early in 1980: 'Those programmes brought huge ratings for RTE. They asked big sporting names like Limerick hurler, Pat Hartigan, Dave O'Leary, swimmer David Cummins, Formula One driver Derek Daly, athlete Noel Carroll, Dublin footballer, Jimmy Keaveney, boxer Mick Dowling and Cork's Jimmy Barry-Murphy to participate. To give a light touch to the proceedings the sports personalities were divided into teams each made up of two "superathletes", one female athlete, one personality and one politician. Personalities who agreed to take part included Fr Michael Cleary, Frank Kelly and Dickie Rock. After he won the competition the previous year Pat Spillane took part in the World Superstars competition in the Bahamas. He did not know much about protecting himself from the sun and as a result of his pink visage and body a new phrase entered popular currency, "Pat Spillane tan"!'

Death of a friend

Events on the footballing field that year were overshadowed by a terrific tragedy off it. John Morley played a then record 112 senior games for the county up to 1974, captaining Mayo to their first Connacht senior title in 12 years, and also starred in 1969 winning side. In the same years he also helped Connacht to Railway Cup successes.

Earley frequently came up against John but his outstanding memory of him was of a match they played together:

'We played together for Connacht and having won the Railway Cup in 1969, we went out to New York to play in the Cardinal Cushing Games. In our first game against New York in Boston, I was playing very well in midfield. On one occasion the ball was hanging in the air. I went into the clouds, or so I thought, to catch the ball. I touched the ball and then it was wrenched from my hands. As I reached the ground, I turned around quickly to be on the defensive, but I looked around to see that it as my teammate John Morley with the ball tucked in as tight as could be, ready to set up another attack. You would have to consider him as being one of the great players.

'The most famous incident in his illustrious career came in the 1970 League final clash when Mayo defeated Down. John was playing at centre-half back, when a Down player grabbed him and tore his shorts. Just as he was about to put his foot into a new shorts, the ball came close by, he abandoned his shorts and in his briefs fielded the ball and cleared it heroically down the field to the adulation of the crowd.

'In the west of Ireland there are two things we are known for. One is for saying "mighty". The other thing we are noted for, is that we generally refer to people we admire, even though we may never have met them, by their surname. If you go into any GAA setting in the West of Ireland today, indeed all the West of Ireland is a GAA setting and you say "Morley", everyone will know the name. He remains known by that name with affection and admiration.'

Inevitably any discussion on John Morley's career is overshadowed by the tragic circumstances of his death. The man who gave every ounce of energy on the playing-field for Mayo, was prepared to put his life on the line to honour his professional duty and uphold law and order regardless of any risk to his personal safety. The bravery which he had so often exhibited in the green and red of Mayo was to manifest itself even more strikingly in the dark blue uniform of the Garda. A hero in life became a hero in death:

'John was murdered on the 7 July 1980 just a few days before the Connacht final with a fellow native of Knock, Henry Byrne. He was just 37 years of age. Another Mayo man and centre-forward for Michael Glaveys, Derek Kelly was injured in the incident. John had initially been based in Ballaghaderreen on the Mayo-Roscommon border before moving to Roscommon town and finally to Castlerea. In all three places he had fully immersed himself in all manner of community activities.

'A robbery had taken place, in a time when the IRA were involved in a campaign to rob banks, and the squad car encountered the getaway car at the crossroads outside Loughlynn on the way to Ballaghaderreen. Shots were fired and Henry Byrne and John Morley were fatally wounded. First on the scene was a retired Garda, the late Garda Kneafsey. Interviewed on the RTE news that night he said he had arrived on the scene to discover a guard wounded and badly bleeding on the side of the road and that he had recognised him immediately as "the footballer". He spoke to him but the man was shaking as if registering arrows of pain shooting through his now frail body. John had said to him, "I'm getting awful cold" which indicated a loss of blood. Then he said an *Act of Contrition.* Shortly after the ambulance arrived, but it was too late to save John.

'The human tragedy had a huge effect on Connacht because the Connacht final was just up the road, the following Sunday. It was between Mayo and Roscommon, between a county that John had played for, and the county he lived in for many years. Everybody in both counties respected him totally. In the circumstances Roscommon's 3-13 to 0-8 hardly seemed to matter.'

That game was memorable for a young Mayo player. T.J. Kilgallon's first taste of success came in 1978 when he was on the Mayo team that beat a star-leaden Dublin side including Barney Rock and Kieran Duff to win the All-Ireland minor final. Two years later he found himself lining out at midfield in the Connacht senior final:

'I was only 18 and it was a real baptism of fire. I was marking Dermot Earley. He wasn't that big but he had massive shoulders and legs and to be honest I was a bit intimidated in his company. They hammered us but Dermot made a point of seeking me out after the game to shake my hand. He was a real gentleman. I think the only player I have seen with stronger legs was Harry Keegan. We played Roscommon in 1983 and Harry shouldered me, completely fairly, but left me completely winded.

'Dermot was a wonderful player. He had so many facets to his game. He was an exceptional fielder, always controlled things very well in the middle of the field, always scored a lot and was deadly from frees. He was a very powerful man on a pitch. He had a perfectionist streak to him: he trained very hard and he looked after himself really well. I doubt if he ever smoked or drank and he was always very fit.

'His athletic body generated astonishing power but, patently, that phenomenon testifies to the even more profound strength of his spirit. He must rank as the greatest player never to win an All-Ireland medal.'

What's another year?

Simply being the best does not of itself guarantee the biggest prize but in 1980 the pieces of the jigsaw seemed to be fitting together nicely for Roscommon. Earley made a point of listening to what is said in the dressing-room. Players revelling in past glories on and especially off the field, bludgeoning their way into the conversation with a half-formed anecdote, growls of assent and of venomous dissent.

Interruptions are occasionally brutal, each voice more insistent, swaggering with sharper instances than its predecessor. Conversations, which are both serious and witty, abound in penetrating insights but it was not about the words. They are merely seamless, enfolded intricacies of vowels and syllables and broken rhythms. It is all about the tone. As the spiritual leader of the team he needed to know the mood of the men, the way they spoke and what was important to them. He had to be good at reading faces. He had to be to appreciate the subtle difference between when a player blinks in acknowledgment and the moments when the lashes touch for a fraction longer, suggesting a softening, a form of encouragement. Then there's the smiles: sometimes bonhomie, but sometimes a strain betrays itself in a smile, like the smile of a deaf person afraid of showing incomprehension, and in the anxious look of his eyes. Above all he had to be constantly alert for glances, which are veiled and hostile when the story is told in the silences. In this close-knit society where every emotional ripple is registered he sensed that 1980 was going to be the year for Roscommon. Their code was: ask not what your teammates can do for you. Ask what you can do for your teammates.

Throughout the team there were players in the peak of their form: Seamus Hayden's willingness to submerge his ego in the role of reliable fetcher and carrier; Danny Murray steaming enterprisingly but sensibly up and down the flanks and John O'Gara's tirelessly inventive running and crisp control and distribution. Whereas in the past there was an elemental rythmn about their play Tom Heneghan brought the tactical sophistication, individually and collectively, to ensure that any kamikaze inclinations would not bring late embarrassment and that the dramatic range of their talents had the freedom to blossom as the creative influence the team's technical virtuosity had long entitled it to be.

Sex in the city

Earley felt the season was pregnant with a promise as palpable as the ticking of a time bomb: 'We had great players and personalities who all brought something different to the squad. We became a band of brothers. Danny Murray won All-Star awards in consecutive years, in 1979 and 1980. He was famous in the squad for his propensity to have a steak for lunch before a big game.

'Probably the great character in the squad was Gerry Emmett. I was always incredibly focused in my preparations not just for games but even for training sessions of the team. Gerry decided to send me a curved ball one day and asked me if he would have sex before a match, expecting an indignant reaction. I decided to turn defence into attack and calmly said: 'Well I might but not if it was a big match. It would slow me down too much. How about yourself?' Gerry went as red as bedroot and for the first time in history was speechless. When he finally regained his composure he cheekily asked how much it would slow me down. I replied: "About 10 seconds."

'It seemed Gerry was the perpetual sub but it never got him down. The Connacht Council had a special celebration for us to mark the anniversary of one of our Connacht titles in McHale Park in Castlebar at half-time. Before the first half finished there was an announcement over the loudspeaker: "Would the 1980 Roscommon team please go the dugout". One of the lads asked: "Where's the dugout?" Quick as a flash Gerry interjected: "I'll show ye. I know every dugout in every county in Ireland."'

Earley took confidence from the blend of youth and experience: 'The spine of the team were very experienced but the new lads brought another dimension. Tom Heneghan did a great job as our manager. He was ahead of his time as a coach. With Tony Mc, Mick Finneran and John O'Connor in our forward line we had three guys who could get you scores. Their worth was really shown in the All-Ireland semi-final in 1980 against Armagh, when after failing in four previous semi-finals we finally qualified for the All-Ireland. Tony's goal that day typified what our forward line was capable of. Tom once said to us: "Our tactics are very simple; get the ball fast into the forwards." There was none of the passing to the side or even backwards that you see today.'

In the build-up to the final Earley's mind never seemed to fully settle down. His ambition had fixed on the Sam Maguire Cup. Two days before the 1980 All-Ireland final, Earley took a break from football by acting as best man at his brother Peter's wedding to Ena Courtney in Castlepollard. One memory in particular endured for him: 'We had a lady photographer who took hours, after the ceremony, to ensure that the photos were right. At one stage she stood on the roof of a car to get the perfect shot. The wind blew her dress high in the air to the amusement of everybody as people were getting bored with all the waiting around.

'At the reception, as I was making my speech and thanking everybody, my mother was prompting me with names of people that I should not forget. Finally she reminded me of the photographer. I said: "My mother is shouting at me not to forget the photographer". To great applause I continued by saying: "Will I ever forget the photographer?"'

Roscommon fans will never forget the night before the All-Ireland final in 1980. Kerry's Jimmy Deenihan was interviewed, by telephone, from the team hotel by Liam O'Murchu on RTE's special *Up for the Match* programme. Liam asked Jimmy: '*An raibh tú ag feachaint ar an clár?*'

He replied: '*Ní raibh. Bhíomar ag feachaint ar Match of the Day.*'

The Roscommon players were watching in at the time and got a great laugh from Jimmy's answer. Sadly it was probably the only laugh they got that weekend.

This is it

The date with destiny finally arrived. In the secret crevices of individual consciousness the tension in the dressing-room reminded Earley of the aftermath of a thunderclap: full of sound and yet intensely silent. Indeed, it seemed this day that he himself hovered in a state of suspension - that he was waiting for something that he could only hardly imagine and was only beginning to be prepared for.

Despite the weather the colour and spirit of the crowd had splintered the dullness of the day. When the Roscommon team ran onto the pitch the fans raised an earsplitting cacophony. The grass was so smooth you could roll marbles across it.

As an army of photographers thronged the pitch the preliminaries just added to the tension. At last the referee was in the middle of the field with his whistle in his mouth. The match that these thirty players had been dreaming about all their lives was just a breath away:

'It was just incredible to reach the All-Ireland final in 1980. Tom had us really well prepared. He arranged for us to get two weeks off work and for those two weeks we trained twice a day, at noon and in the early evening. By night time you couldn't wait to get to bed. We had Kerry reeling early on but I feel we lost because we weren't attacking enough. We had great attacking half-backs and on the day they did a good defensive job but we didn't use them to attack Kerry. Offaly beat Kerry in 1982 by attacking them. We had the class to do the same but we didn't.

'We were gutted afterwards especially for the supporters. They gave us a massive reception when we got home. Every year Roscommon plays in the Connacht Championship there's an expectation that we can do something significant. The Roscommon supporters really rally behind the team as was shown in Ennis in 2006 when Roscommon beat Kerry in the replay of the All-Ireland minor final. The atmosphere was incredible and judging by the massive traffic jam on the way home from the game, every man, woman and child in the county was at the game. That Roscommon team played football the way I think it should be played: with great support play, no fouling and enormous commitment.'

For Harry Keegan the disappointment was intense: 'What stays with me is that there was no real celebration from the Kerry players nor the fans. That's what hurt me the most. Winning had become so routine it didn't seem to matter to them. When they won in 1997 you could see it did matter to the Kerry lads because they hadn't won an All-Ireland for 11 years at that stage.'

Like a leading racehorse that has been carefully hard-held into the straight, Kerry had quickened and left the opposition standing. In the end Kerry's flood of talent and feeling was enough to sweep them through the hostile gauntlet of the Roscommon defence and to claim the crown that was theirs by right.

The Kerry team shared a sense of the immutable bond that victory brings, a feeling of kinship that goes beyond professional loyalty, a camaraderie that overcomes differences of age, sex, even previous fallings out. Seamus Heaney was wrong. Eroticism is not the first taste of the transcendent. Winning an All-Ireland is.

The Roscommon fans were irate about the refereeing of the game. Legend has it that one of them approached the referee immediately after the game and said, 'Hi ref, How's your dog?'

The ref is said to have replied, 'What do you mean? I don't have a dog.'

The fan responded, 'That's strange. You're the first blind man I've ever met that doesn't have a guide dog!'

That evening a convoy of cars and buses made their way home. The normal buzz of chat and banter was noticeably absent. One of the songs that came on the radio was the big smash from Abba at the time: *The Winner Takes It All.*

Those five words said it all.

The winner takes it all

A bitter raking over the ashes is pointless. That day Dermot took the field, tall and powerfully upright, ready to set the match alight with tenacious runs. In the script he had written it in his head there was not to be a desperate scramble of shots at goal at the end with few were reaching the target or frees spinning away on an aimless trajectory. In 1992 I asked Dermot to write a review of the 1980 All-Ireland. It went as follows:

This was not a great All-Ireland final. Both sets of defenders were well on top and scoring chances were at a premium. Marking was extremely close and this resulted in too many frees from each team but it as not a dirty game. However, many of the decisions left the players bewildered, not to mention the crowd. Roscommon suffered more than Kerry in this area.

We became frustrated and our game suffered as a result. Kerry deserved to win because they took their chances well. We had the winning of the game from placed balls alone but the concentration slipped and so did the opportunity for victory.

Each time I have looked at the game, I experience an excitement that I know should not be there but is brought on by the occasion of the final and that there will unfold before me the missed opportunities of scores and chances lost that would have made us All-Ireland champions.

I was disappointed that Eoin Liston did not play as it was a shame for any footballer to miss the All-Ireland final for any reason, but particularly for ill-health. We felt all along we could have beaten Kerry with him because in Pat Lindsay we had a full-back who could have held him.

The start was magic – a goal from John O'Connor followed by sustained pressure from Roscommon and a further point from Seamus Hayden. Then Kerry took over and threw the ball around but our defence was good. Gerry Connellan and Mike Sheehy appear to be booked by the referee and then Tommy Doyle and I got our names taken. This happened as Kerry came forward. I turned hard to the left to follow the attack and bumped hard into the back of a Kerry player. He turned and let me have one in the face. The ref called us together as I got off the ground. The Kerry man was my former army colleague, Tommy Doyle. The referee booked me. I asked him: "Why are you booking me ref?" He said nothing. He booked Doyle then moved away. Tommy and I looked at one another. We shook hands. There were no hard feelings but I was disappointed to be booked in my first All-Ireland final. Micheál O'Hehir in his commentary said: "Tommy was a lucky man, he wasn't sent to the side-line," but then the referee decided to hop the ball and O'Hehir wondered who hit who. Now I got frustrated as I felt doubly punished, booked and lost a free to a hop ball.

Roscommon got going again and John O'Gara hit a good point from 50 yards. It was 1-2 to 0-0 with 12 minutes gone. They got a goal and two points. We moved forward again and Mick Finneran was penalized for holding the ball too long. We regained the lead when I pointed a 50 and then Harry Keegan was penalised for a foul on John Egan. Nobody knew for what, as he had cleanly and with great skill, turned, trapped the ball with his left foot and let Egan run by. More frustration. Mike Sheehy points a free a few moments later – level again. There were no further scores in the first-half but a few incidents did occur. Firstly, the linesman called for the attention of the referee and they both went to the Roscommon dug-out. Play was help up. We had the wind and we didn't want to waste time. Tom Heneghan was told to stay in the dug-out. Mick O'Dwyer was up on the line for much of the first half and nothing was said to him. Time was being wasted and selective justice was administered – more frustration.

Jimmy Deenihan won a free under the Cusack Stand. The free was taken and as Roscommon won the ball, the referee halted play as Mick O'Dwyer was on the side-line with substitute Ger O'Driscoll. It looked as if O'Driscoll was being introduced. The referee went to the line and discussed the situation with O'Dwyer. O'Driscoll was not introduced. The free was retaken. Roscommon did not win the ball that time. More frustration.

Gerry Fitzmaurice and Pat Spillane were involved in an incident off the ball. It was also off-screen. Pat was on the ground and took an age to get up. Time went by and many efforts were made to assist his recovery, to no avail. Eventually he staggered up. Both players appeared to be booked and play resumed with a hop ball. Micheál O'Hehir wondered: "Is Pat Spillane really hurt or is he in line for an Oscar?" Much time had been wasted again.

Thirty seven minutes after the ball was thrown in at the start of the game the first half ended. Two minutes of extra time was played. Spillane must have been down for about four minutes not to mention the other stoppages. It was 1-3 all and now we had to face the wind.

The final score was 1-9 to 1-6. Kerry won and deservedly so, before a crowd of 63,854. As I pondered the result it stood out that the difference between the teams was Mike Sheehy's accurate free taking. He scored six frees and a goal from play. Although Roscommon scored 1-4 from play to Kerry's 1-3, we missed frees we should have scored.

Our defence was magnificent, all six of them, but so were Kerry's rearguard. The midfield was even enough with both set of midfielders on top at different times but O'Shea and Walsh probably shaded it a little. The closeness of the contest in each section of the field accounted for some of the frees but whereas much physical contact took place from both sides all through, it was not a dirty game. Yes, after a marvellous start, Roscommon seemed to change their style of play as the openings which were there in the first few minutes were quickly closed off by the

Top gun

Star in stripes: Dermot takes office as Chief of Staff in 2007.

Simply the Best: Dermot tackles George Best in a charity match.

Thou shalt not pass: Roscommon's Pat Lindsay (left) and Harry Keegan (right) thwart Dublin's Kieran Duff.

Kicking king: Dermot Earley in action for Roscommon in July, 1985.

The boss

In the hot seat: Dermot becomes Roscommon manager in 1992 (above); and as Kildare boss in 1994.

It's a long way from Roscommon to here: Dermot on a trip to Kosovo in 2008 (above and right).

Rallying the troops

Listen up lads: Dermot adresses the troops.

Foreign parts: Dermot meets troops in Lebanon.

Snow white: Kevin McStay prepares for Dermot Earley's visit to Kosovo. Below: Dermot meets the troops in chilly Kosovo.

A quick word: Dermot and colleagues make final preparations.

Family and friends

Proud parents: Mary and Dermot with Noelle at her graduation in 2006.

With a little help from my friends: Dermot with former teammate Gerry Fitzmaurice in New York in 2006.

Two of the greats: Dermot with Kerry great Mike Sheehy at the Cancer West Golf Classic in Galway.

Kerry defensive unit. I have explained this change of play many times as a self-conscious feeling that Kerry would whittle down our early lead. What happened was that the fear of losing overcame the will to win. Roscommon were not dirty.

I was extremely disappointed when I saw the number of times I fouled an opponent in this game. It was always my policy never to foul and if I did foul during the course of a game I resolved afterwards to play more skilfully and dispossess my opponent rather than foul him. In this All-Ireland final I stretched a jersey and grabbed at a ball in the hands of Seán Walsh but to mention two examples. I can only explain that the fear of losing dictated that my opponent would not be allowed go free and set up a move or score. I did not go out with the intention of fouling and did not realise until I saw the game recently for the first time in 12 years that I had fouled a number of times during the game. The fact that this game took place 12 years ago does not diminish my disappointment at committing these fouls. The lesson at the end was that Mike Sheehy punished our fouls. We did not punish Kerry's.

My feeling of emptiness was almost overwhelming. I can remember turning around and shaking hands with Seánie Walsh. I remember Ger Power being close by and there was a clap on the back and a smile. I turned around immediately because I was absolutely shattered and completely disappointed and I then walked to the dressing-room. Seán Kilbride who was a sub on the team that day caught me by the arm, I looked around and realised that the disappointment was there but you had to get on with your life and had to do things correctly.

Earley saw the aftermath of the All-Ireland final as the beginning of the end for that Roscommon team: 'The thing that disappointed me most was that although we had been a very close unit in the build-up to the final everyone went their separate ways afterwards. Some of the players returned some did not. I remember saying to Mary as we travelled back on the bus: "We should all be together." We had stopped being a team. We were never really together as a unit again.

'Although we got back to Croke Park the next year for the League final, the spirit we had in 1980 was gone. There were huge changes in attitude, preparation, procedures and personnel. The difference was really shown up when we went out in the first round of the championship against Sligo. Looking back now, I think the rot set in the evening of the All-Ireland final when we failed to stick together.'

The Hangover

If 1980 was bad for Earley then 1981 would be even worse as Roscommon, having lost heavily to Galway in the National League final: 'Our League final performance was pathetic. There was a panic reaction to it rather than building on the strengths of the previous year. The drastic changes that were made afterwards caused doubts about the team and that was a significant factor in our defeat.

'I did not think the writing was on the wall, but I felt the wrong decisions were made. I thought the mistakes would not be fatal but that the Sligo match would highlight them and we could learn from them. I expressed my strong reservations, privately, to Tom Heneghan. I felt that if we were to be successful we needed to bring new blood on the team but that was not happening. We did not go in hungry enough against Sligo. Complacency was the major reason we lost.

'When I got back to our dressing-room there was stony silence. It was the worst dressing-room I was ever in. Nobody spoke. They just stared ahead. Any words that day, no matter how magnificent and glorious, would have been lost. I can see the dressing-room now. People were sitting with their hands down or with their heads between their legs, gear half-off, boots still on, jerseys on the floor. I shook hands with Pat Lindsay and that was all I could do.'

The delight of sport is its sheer unpredictability. Bit players rise to the occasion when star performers have buckled under the burden of expectation. Such journeymen are addicted to the lure of upstaging the greats for just one day. Harry Keegan pulls no punches when giving the reasons for Roscommon's fall from grace when they lost to Sligo in the Connacht Championship: 'Sligo was a disaster. I was very annoyed with certain players, with a few of the forwards who were not right nor focused. I knew from events beforehand that some of our players we depended the most on were not up for the game the way Sligo were. At that stage we needed to get some new blood coming into the team but we had no new talent coming through.'

Earley produced one of his finest ever performances for Roscommon later that November in the defeat of Kerry in the National League. The following Friday he was doing a course for army officers. They were briefed by a press-officer. He stressed repeatedly that army officers should not seek publicity.

At lunch-time the *Irish Independent* was circulated. The 'Sport star of the Week' was none other than Dermot Earley. All his class-mates ganged up on him and informed him that he was in breach of army rules!

Time to Stay Goodbye

No player can defy Father Time. If a week is a long time in politics then a year can be a lifetime sport, especially when you are on the wrong side of 30, and carrying recurring injuries. In 1985 Earley had clearly stated that he would retire from inter-county football at the end of the Championship the golden glow that surrounded him for so long seemed to have dimmed a little.

The final curtain came in a bad beating to a Mayo team brimming with gifted young players like Kevin McStay in the Connacht final. Driven by the old universal craving to see inspired excellence get it's due the Mayo team in an incredible gesture of sportsmanship carried Earley shoulder high off the field. This vignette contained the essence of Mayo's football tradition, its beauty and *élan* and undiluted joy. The great teams really thrill us and make us respect them.

It was a spontaneous, marvellously unforced gesture, utterly characteristic of a group of players whose resilience perfectly represent the irresistible qualities of a game which, at its best, is one of the most natural and enchanting metaphors for life that sport has to offer. From an early age they had learned, and went on relearning, how to live not only with losing but with losing painfully. Now it was their turn to enter the Promised Land of Croke Park.

It was oddly fitting that Earley's football career ended against the green and red. His own story began in Mayo.

4

The Master

WE do not choose the things we believe in. They choose us.

To understand Dermot Earley the man it is necessary to understand his relationship with his father. Even at his lowest moment his Dad could strike a positive note: 'My father came into the dressing-room with my young brother Paul after we lost the All-Ireland to Kerry in 1980. The first words he said to me were: "There will be next year."

'His only comment on the match was that we had missed many chances that I should have taken the frees. One of the things that he would always do when I played an important game, or went abroad with the army was to take out a silver coin and spit on it and wish me luck. He did that on the morning of the final. He did the same thing in 1982 when I saw him for the last time as I headed off on a peace-keeping mission abroad. Just as he had offered words of encouragement to me as an eight-year-old, there he was with me in the worst moment of my sporting life with a positive message: "Next year."'

'My abiding memory of my father is of a day we came were coming home from a day in the bog when I was in my late teens. He turned to me and said: "You know you and me are like brothers, not like father and son."

'My father believed that reading is to the mind what exercise is to the body. The picture in my head I always have of him is of him reading a book, invariably about history. That was his characteristic pose.'

The green and red of Mayo

It was a time when marriage was for richer or poorer - or the land. When the first child of Mr. and Mrs. Peadar Earley was born in Castlebar on 24 February in 1948 football fans in Roscommon could have not foreseen that this birth would have such significance for their football fortunes in years to come.

Peadar Earley was an only child. His father died when he was two and his mother when he was 13. From then on family friends reared him. He was a scholarship boy winning a scholarship to St Gerard's College for his secondary education and then to the De La Salle training college in Waterford where he qualified as a national teacher. His first posting was in Limerick but he returned a year later to his native Mayo to take up a teaching post there. An important consideration in the move was that it allowed him to be close to his sweetheart Katherine (Kitty) Byrne. Her family owned a pub in Main Street, Castlebar. They also had an egg exporting licence. One of Earley's most vivid childhood memories is of being surrounded by an ocean of eggs in a massive shed where they were packaged for export.

Dermot always spoke evocatively of a childhood that had vanished. In this environment everyone had no choice but to learn the virtues of thrift and stoicism at an early age. Poverty, even relative poverty, makes you clever. Without some ingenuity you do not eat all the time, and so you have to be smart. Potatoes are peeled slowly and methodically with a small paring knife, leaving as little potato on the peel as possible. These were simple things but look after the pennies and the pounds take care of themselves.

The Earley family lived in a rented house in Cruck outside Balla. In 1953 they moved to Cloonbonniffe outside Castlerea where Peadar took up his appointment as principal. The attraction of the school was that there was a good chance that a house would come available which would serve as the teacher's house on a permanent basis.

It was here that Dermot's football education began when his father taught him how to kick a football. It was only a small brown rubber ball but the rudiments of all of the skills of the game were learnt using that ball.

By this time the Earley family was expanding rapidly. A year and a day after Dermot was born came Denise and after that came Margaret and two sons Peter and Paul.

For seven year-old Dermot Earley the house had two main attractions. It was right beside a shop which meant that it was easy to buy lollipops. There was also a big garden attached which was ideal for playing football.

In 1956 Peadar Earley founded Gorthaganny GAA club. The club was called after Michael Glavey who was killed in an attack on Ballinlough RIC Barracks on September 14, 1920. He fed his eldest son a diet of football legend and lore: 'Football left him with a wealth of happy memories. He once told me about one of his first club games as a minor. At that stage it was hard to field a team. There was one guy roped into play for them and he was provided with boots, socks, a jersey, the lot. They were thrashed and of course when that happens everybody blames everybody else. When unflattering comments were put to the new recruit, his riposte was, "Well you can't blame me. I never got near the ball!"

Peadar was a great admirer of the pride people took in playing club football and told a story to illustrate it. Within hours of the tragic death of the corner-forward in a traffic accident, an ambitious young hopeful rang the local club chairman. 'I hope you don't mind me ringing at this time,' he said, 'But I was wondering whether I might take the place of the deceased . . .'

'I hadn't really thought about it,' replied the chairman, 'but if the undertaker doesn't mind, then neither will I.'

The Earley family had to pay a price for young Dermot's football fanaticism. One day they were all gathering for the dinner. His sister Denise was calling in her big brother for his meal but was being ignored as he continued to kick the football up again the wall as if his life depended on it. His mother had put all the food on the table and was not prepared to tolerate any more delay. She ran outside to tell her son that he had to come in for his dinner in the most emphatic manner. The response she got was: "Just one more kick." The kick shattered the glass in the window beside the dinner table. Not a single scrap of food could be saved. It would be a bread and jam lunch instead of a hot meal.

Every Face Tells A Story

As Earley's every wakening moment seemed to go into football his mother became increasingly distressed that his exploits in sport were hampering his progress in school. One night he was given an ultimatum: 'More of the books, less of the boots.'

Before every match she gave her son the same advice: 'Don't get hurt and don't hurt anybody.' Invariably she would make the same response every time he came home with a sad face. She would ask: 'Did ye win?' The facial expression would say everything and she would give her standard answer to her own question: 'No. What harm.'

Even when her son's career was at its zenith she would not attend matches. She would travel but would spend her time in the Church: 'I could never bear watching either Dermot or Paul playing. I was terrified they would hurt themselves. If either of them got hurt I was never told. In 1985 somebody asked me was Dermot better. It was only then that I discovered that Dermot had broken his jaw in a match a few weeks earlier.'

Apart from safety her primary concern was that her son would look well on the pitch. This was a difficult task.

As a 10-year-old Earley asked his father if it would be possible to buy a pair of togs. They went to Castlebar and spent 10 shillings, a small fortune, on a pair of togs. They were much too big for him, going down below his knees and almost up to his shoulders. All his friends had a great laugh at him but he did not mind. He had a pair of togs of his own. Now he was a real player.

As he played on his own in the garden he wore a Glaveys' jersey. The chairman of the club passed by at one stage and told him he was no good of a footballer unless he had his togs dirty. Immediately young Earley went into the neighbour's field and sat in a cow dung.

Twenty minutes later the chairman passed by again. This time he shouted in that Earley was a great player because he had dirty togs. His mother was less than pleased at the smell and the dirt, which ensued.

After getting his first pair of togs Earley was panic-struck when he saw that his mother was using a sewing needle on them. He was terrified that something had torn them. His anxiety abated when he discovered that all she was doing was sewing on a miraculous medal to them. Up to the time of his marriage every pair of togs he wore had some kind of holy medal attached.

A tense moment arose between mother and son when Dermot decided to change his diet. He heard a story that the top English soccer players ate raw liver to give them additional strength. One day Earley sneaked into the kitchen and helped himself to half the liver. It was very difficult to digest and tasted ghastly but he figured it was a small price to pay for such a worthy cause. Some time later he evacuated his house with the speed of light when he heard his mother shouting from the kitchen over the sound of eggs sizzling in grease: 'What happened to my liver?'

Kitty Earley glowed visibly as she talked about her eldest son. Her memories centered on Dermot's relationship with his father: 'Dermot never seemed to be at home. He was always either out in the fields kicking ball, farming with the neighbours or off with his dad. They were very close. Dermot got his father's temperament. Both of them got on very well with people, but I would say Dermot is stricter with his children than his father was.

'Dermot could do no wrong in his father's eyes. Now and again somebody would say Dermot had a terrible match. Peadar would always say: "Ah no. He wasn't that bad."

Armed with his father's stature and his mother's nature Dermot appreciated his mother's influence on him more with each passing year: 'I suppose I inherited many of my mother's characteristics and qualities, fierce independence, a near obsession with punctuality, a concern to use money judiciously, a deep attraction to privacy and a belief that a promise made should not be broken. Whenever it was necessary she had no hesitation in bringing me down a peg or two, but criticism was always tactfully offered. In the cossetted comfort of her presence I learned much about patience, kindness, and selflessness.'

Educating Dermot

Although Earley appreciated what he learned from the scouts it paled into insignificance when compared to his pleasure at what he learned from his father. It was an era of corporal punishment but Peadar Earley was not given to extremes of violence. Yet he was strong enough to use any hint of a threat to his authority to proclaim publicly his word was Holy Writ. In those moments the strength of his command would activate a seismograph. The pupils knew he was not a man to trifle with when he was intense and not inclined to be garrulous and in the moments when a glacial sternness came over his features.

As an enterprising teacher Peadar Earley capitalised on all the interest in football by using the football one day as a teaching aid. He was trying to explain about latitude and longitude and used a piece of chalk on a brown ball to draw lines from the North pole to the South pole. Decades on this lesson was still remembered by his son: 'I am an expert on latitude and longitude because of that lesson. All our eyes were riveted on the ball. If any of us had gone into metrology or shipping we would have had a head start.'

Apart from his teaching duties and his football work Peadar was actively involved in community life: 'He had been involved in the campaign to get a graveyard for the area. I remember watching *Hall's Pictorial Weekly* and seeing Frank Hall read out a headline from the *Roscommon Champion*: "People in Gorthaganny are dying for a graveyard.'

As 'the master' he was the most educated person in the parish apart from the priest. In an era when most adults in rural Ireland, particularly elderly people, had very little education, Peadar's services were eagerly sought after by people who were applying for pensions or who had formal letters to write.

Train of thought

Earley was ecstatic at what he learned through attending football matches with his father. His earliest such memory is of a trip to Castlebar: 'It was the first football pitch I ever saw. On a Saturday evening in the early '50's, before a Connacht championship game, my late father took me out to McHale Park. I was about four years old at the time and we were living in Castlebar.

'Later on came another vivid memory of going to a match with him. It was the great Seán Purcell's final Championship game with Galway. Daddy always believed that he was the greatest player in the history of the game. We witnessed an incident, which has become part of GAA folklore. In the 1962 Connacht final Roscommon trailed Galway by five points with less than 10 minutes to go and looked like a beaten side. A Galway forward took a shot and put his team six points up. As the ball was cutting like a bullet over the crossbar, the Roscommon goalie, the late Aidan Brady, a big man, jumped up and hung on the crossbar and it broke.

'There was a lengthy delay until a new crossbar was found. The delay disrupted Galway's rhythm and allowed Roscommon to snatch victory thanks to a vintage display by Gerry O'Malley.

'I remember talking to Gerry later about it. He said to me: "I thought it probably had gone from us at that stage and we wouldn't be able to turn it around." Then he went to midfield and they got two goals to tie things up. When they equalisied Gerry ran over to the Roscommon fans who were on the sideline and asked them how much time was left. They said that time was up. He won the ball and put Des Feeley through for the winning point.'

Dermot also inherited some of his father's eating habits: 'Although he was the most unfussy eater I have ever known, Daddy's one great culinary weakness was mushrooms. He would wake me up early in the mornings during August and I would go out mushroom-picking under the warm glow of the rising sun while he started gathering cows for the milking. Under his tutelage I learned quickly that most valuable skill for any practitioner of my new profession - how to tell a field which would yield mushrooms from one which would not. Once in a blue moon I would reach treasure island - a seemingly limitless, just-popped bunch of pure-white mushrooms lovingly caressing the green grass.'

Yes. Yes. Yes

In all of the matches they watched together his father would always draw attention to facets of the game, which his son should pay particular attention to, and learn from. The benefits of acting on his father's advice was dramatically highlighted one summer's evening:

'It was at half-time in a West Roscommon juvenile match that I was asked can you kick with your left-foot. Glavey's were playing Ballinagare and were losing by a big score. The game was being played in Loughlynn in the field by the lake and John Gallagher was organising the team at half-time. He placed the goalie, backs and midfield and then looked around for forwards. I was closest to him, looking in awe, and he caught me by the arm and said: "Can you kick with your left foot?" My heart beat faster than ever before and I said yes. "Left half-forward", he shouted and pushed me into a position - I was on the team at the tender age of eight and a half. I got three kicks at the ball (one blocked down) but I did not care. My Dad was proud of me but not as proud as I was of myself. It was the beginning of a way of life. I am eternally grateful to John for grabbing me by the arm and also to my father who had encouraged me to practise with my left foot. In order to be good, he said, you must kick with both feet. Because of him I was able to play my first game with Glaveys.'

Peadar Earley took every available opportunity to broaden his son's horizons. A big event in the Earley household was the purchase of their first radio. When Peadar brought the radio home on his bicycle the family wanted him to assemble it and try it out immediately. However, the operation had to be put on ice for three hours as Dermot was gone off playing football. His father would not hear of doing anything with the radio until he arrived back.

The radio brought a major change not just in the Earley family but in the village as a whole because they were one of the first families to have a radio in the locality. A neighbour was calling around to visit the house the night they got the radio but refused to come in because of all the strange voices. Every Sunday the GAA fans in the area would converge onto the Earley household to hear commentaries of matches on the radio.

In the 1930s the GAA entered a new era with the emergence of the greatest evangelist since Saint Paul. In 1938, Mícheál O'Hehir made his first GAA commentary at the Galway-Monaghan All-Ireland football semi-final in Mullingar:

'Growing up there were few distractions apart from the wireless with the wet batteries and dry batteries and of course we listened to O'Hehir's commentaries religiously. Listening to the radio we never saw those great players but Micheál, who really made the GAA, turned them into superheroes.

'Mícheál O'Hehir was the man who brought Gaelic games in vivid form to the people of Ireland at a time when television was unknown and transistors unheard of. He was a national institution. As we march, not always successfully, to the relentless demands of a faster, more superficial age just to hear his voice was to know that all was well with the world. He painted pictures with words like a master craftsman. Young boys listening to him decided immediately they wanted to join the ranks of the football and hurling immortals. Irish sport is not the same without him. He was irreplaceable. Nobody ever did more for the GAA than him.'

The weekend matches provoke intense discussion. Great sporting moments were dissected here with an insight and lyricism that Neville Cardus would have been proud off. Old controversies emerged from their caves of obscurity and were delicately excavated.

Even if supporters of county teams are sometimes united by a shared error about their ancestry and a general loathing of their neighbours fans are the lifeblood of the GAA. In 1962 Roscommon's best-known fan Paddy Joe Burke was listening to his first ever All-Ireland semi-final in the family kitchen with half their neighbours in attendance, as was the norm in rural Ireland. His beloved Roscommon were trailing Cavan. Disaster struck when the batteries died temporarily and the commentary was lost. Paddy Joe's mother intervened immediately and told everyone to get on their knees and say the rosary. Such was the power of the their prayers that when the rosary was finished not alone was the radio working but Roscommon had taken the lead and went on to win the match.

A Shattering Experience

As in every thing else in young Dermot Earley's life, his choice of secondary school was determined by football considerations. He chose to become a boarder in St Nathy's College, Ballaghadreen in 1960 because they had won the Hogan Cup (the All-Ireland colleges senior final) in 1957 and were beaten finalists in 1959.

The regime in St Nathy's was very strict. Parents were not allowed on the school premises during term. On Earley's first Sunday in the college he ran outside the gates where his father was waiting to hear all the news. His father was in for a shock because Dermot told him that he was going to play in the juvenile trial but would talk to him when it was over. An hour and a half later Dermot came out panting.

Study started five minutes later. His father had made a round trip of 20 miles on his bicycle for less than 10 minutes of conversation. Nonetheless he returned home a contented man. His son was settling satisfactorily in his new school and had acquitted himself well in the juvenile trials.

Earley's first appearance in the St Nathy's colours was memorable for the wrong reason. They lost by 7-7 to no score. It was at Nathys that Roscommon's second ever All-Star became a lifelong friend with Sligo's second ever All-Star winner, as Barnes Murphy recalls: 'Our star was Dermot Earley though in his first match we lost by a huge score. He never changed one iota since then. As a result of going to school with him I always felt I could hold my own against him. In a match he would often get a dig in the ribs but he would never hit you back. The most he would ever do would be to ask you why you did it.'

In Earley's five years in St Nathy's the biggest footballing thorn in their side was St Jarlath's College, Tuam in general and their star player, Jimmy Duggan, in particular. They regularly thwarted Nathy's ambitions in the Connacht championship at all grades. The only exceptions were in 1963 when Earley captained the juvenile team to the Connacht title and 1965 when he captained the junior side to championship glory.

Earley also made a big impression on the college basketball scene though he missed out on selection on the international under-age sides because of his football commitments.

One of the biggest handicaps of boarding school life at the time was that pupils were deprived of access to newspapers and radio. This created a lot of problems for the sports fanatics. One night in 1964 the whole dorm engaged in illicit activity by listening to the classic Cassius Clay-Sonny Liston fight.

However, Earley's most enduring memory of his time in college is the day he discovered that his father did not have the full truth on every issue: 'I had total and unreserved respect for him. I felt he was totally infallible. It was a grave disappointment to me to discover for the first time that he was not totally right about everything. I was absolutely devastated.

'I expected everybody else to have the exact same respect for him as I did. I remember once a man coming to our house who asked me to give a message to my "auld fella". I refused because he had called my father an "auld fella". I was furious that he could have such little respect for such a great man.'

A Passionate Priest

News of young Earley's performances reached the ears of the Roscommon minor selectors. He was picked for a challenge match against Westmeath minors in 1963 when he was just 15. His opponent was running rings around him and scoring at will. At one point in the game a high ball came into the Roscommon square. Earley lunged desperately for it accidentally striking his tormentor in the solar plexus with his elbow. His opponent went down like a sack of potatoes and was knocked out cold.

The Roscommon minor selectors were happy with his performance. Even though he had been completely outclassed at least he had the capacity to 'look after' the main threat to the Roscommon goal. Accordingly he was retained for the Connacht minor semi-final against Leitrim. After their final training session before the game the team congregated in a cafe in Roscommon. Fr Pat Brady, whose brother Aidan is rated as one of the greatest goalkeepers of all time, was the team coach and he gave a lengthy talk on the tactics for the game. He made extensive use of the blackboard to illustrate the main points of his instructions.

Fr Brady's final words took the team by surprise: 'I am living up there on the Leitrim border and I am sick to death hearing what Leitrim are going to do to Roscommon next Sunday. When ye have beaten Leitrim by 5 goals and 65 points would ye ever kick the skittering football up their skittering arses.'

There was stunned silence. This was very *Avant garde* language from a priest in 1963. After what seemed like an eternity somebody laughed. Within 30 seconds the whole team had collapsed with laughter. Somebody whispered: 'By God. He is an awful man.'

Roscommon did beat Leitrim but not by the score Fr Brady specified only to lose to Mayo in the Connacht final. Apart from

Earley the other player on the team who would play a major role in Roscommon football in years to follow was Tom Heneghan, who scored a goal from a penalty in the Connacht final.

The disappointment at losing the Connacht final was quickly forgotten as Michael Glaveys won the Roscommon juvenile final. Apart from county medals the prize for winning was a trip to Croke Park for the All-Ireland final courtesy of a cigarette company who took a juvenile side from a different county each year. The whole team headed off on a bus to see Dublin beat Galway in the final. It was a feast for the senses: a mix of fun, fiesta, magic and glamour.

The One That Got Away

Two years later Earley was back in Croke Park again only this time as a player. As Connacht minor champions, and bewitched by the success, Roscommon played Derry in the All-Ireland semi-final. It was a significant weekend for Earley because his Leaving Cert results were out the day before the game. He headed for Dublin with the rest of the team as the results were being made available. He was not going to jeopardise his preparations for the game by waiting around for a piece of paper. That night Michael O'Callaghan congratulated all the players on the panel who had done their Leaving Cert because they had all passed:

'Looking back now I doubt very much if he had contacted all the schools involved to see if we had all passed our exams. However, I was delighted he said those words because it helped me to relax.'

Roscommon played well only to lose by 4-8 to 4-5. The turning point in the match was when Earley missed a penalty: 'I hit the ball as hard as I could. It rose high for the top right hand corner but as it got closer to the goal it started to tail badly wide. I fell prostrate on the ground. I had never felt such devastation up to that moment.'

The following day it was back to Gorthaganny. He was still in a slump of depression. Not even confirmation of his Leaving Cert results raised a ghost of a smile.

Kitty Earley remembered the night well: 'I have never seen Dermot so quiet as he was after that game. We could hardly get a word out of him. It took him days to get over it. I know he lost bigger games after that but that's the one that stands out in my mind as his worst moment.'

That night his father tried to give him a lift by pointing out that he was now part of an elite group of players who had missed a penalty in Croke Park. He rattled off a list of illustrious players who had suffered the same fate. Whatever about the company Earley had joined he still felt absolutely miserable.

Straight from the heart

To really know Dermot Earley it was necessary to walk with him through the fields of Gorthaganny. His childhood is fenced around these fields where in the summer the country air comes thick with fragrant and invisible pollen. Each field conveys a human history. In fact the corner of one field had been used as a mass grave for children during the time of the Great Famine. Up to the 1950s it was used to bury unbaptised babies because the Catholic Church did not at the time allow such children to be buried in consecrated ground. There was just a clump of ferns growing over it. In 2008 Dermot returned to unveil a memorial to their memory: 'These children were denied dignity in life. This monument gives them a little dignity in death.'

Every time he walked these fields Dermot became entangled in the clinging cobwebs of childhood. In the softness of the western mist as he walked these fields from which his heart could never be departed he felt fully at home. In an intensely personal drama this land opened questions about his history and identity, seamlessly woven through the fabric of his life, and went even further to some secret compass point which directed him to somewhere he did not know - crossing boundaries where sadness and pain met so dramatically. As he walked in these fields he tried to listen to its secrets of lives gained and lives lost, strange riches and sadness. It has music of its own. The melody, which entered his consciousness, was a tune of loneliness, poignant cries of quiet despair. In these fields people long dead live again, somehow speaking to years that belong to people not yet born.

The ghost of Dermot Earley will always linger in these fields. His spirit will always live on in his children – some of whom were to make their own splashes on the sporting fields.

5

In The Name Of The Father

A LITANY of woes. Close calls. Demoralising trouncings. For 32 years that was the story of Connacht football. A procession of 'what-might-have-beens'. Galway in '83, 14 against Dublin's 12 and still a defeat. A match that 20 years later can only be whispered about and the video is hidden away forever. The definitive video nasty. A sucker goal given away to Barney Rock and a series of spectacular wides, when it always seemed much, much easier to score. A story exacerbated by repetition, no longer remembered as much as incanted like a prayer got by heart. The gods tended to write depressing scenarios for fans west of the Shannon. A history of disillusion shared by a whole generation. Each defeat remembered, like beads on a rosary.

This was a time when the most Connacht football could hope for was sympathy.

For 32 years it seemed that Gaelic football was hopelessly ill-equipped to carry the burden of emotional expression that Westerners seek to unload upon it. What hurt for so long was that something we believed to be a metaphor for our pride was all along a metaphor for our desperation.

Connacht's reign of error reached its nadir in the 1993 All-Ireland semi-final as Mayo capitulated completely to Cork as they stopped playing and Cork stuffed them by 5-15 to 0-10. We couldn't bear to watch. Yet we couldn't tear our eyes from it like watching a bad traffic accident, torn as we were between passionate partisanship and the knowledge that here was a lost cause - wondering if the inevitable beating would become a butchering. In the finite continuum of time along which all fans of Connacht football travel, this terrible moment is fixed, immovable, incapable of being blotted out, however fervently or passionately we later wished for this erasure. In a fog of self-disgust a legion of

Connacht fans had learned the hard way that to falter is to be swept aside. It was written into the nation's consciousness that Connacht football did not merit serious consideration.

Alas and well may Erin weep
when Connacht lies in slumber deep

The appointment of John O'Mahony as Galway manager in October '97 would change all that. He had qualities that were hard to define but easy to recognise. A man of self-reliance, of candour, he was not a prisoner of the uncertainties, nor the enforced servility of the previous decades. Yet nobody predicted the benign revolution was at hand. Our news values dictates that David Beckham's sarong-wearing habits are more likely to grab the headlines than the plight of a generally mild-mannered school teacher on the Roscommon-Mayo border. O'Mahony had been great at making teams good but would he be good enough to make this Galway team great?

Within 12 months he had taken his side to an All-Ireland final. Galway captain Ray Silke said in the dressing-room before he led his team out: 'Right lads. I'm going out to win an All-Ireland. Who's coming with me?'

True grit

In this patchwork quilt of a game that contained many bright colours things did not look promising for most of the first half. When Dermot Earley scored a goal for Kildare the Galway fans, drawn into the vortex of a furious expense of nervous energy, felt sick with contradictory, unarticulated emotion. They were beginning to feel an almost superstitious foreboding. These lost souls on the highway of life were driven downwards through failure after failure, fate was becoming real to them as a cold malignant force. This was a Connacht team that could win things: but would they let the title slip through their fingers yet again? Was it really true that you had to lose an All-Ireland before you could win one? One of John O'Mahony's favourite maxims was now to come into play, 'A winner never quits. A quitter never wins.'

Eugene McGee incurred the wrath of Galway fans when he spoke of the 'fancy Dans' on O'Mahony's side but in the second half display the Westerners produced a display of dazzling virtuosity with Ja Fallon masterfully orchestrating events. Heroes emerged all over the field with Tomás Mannion, Seán Og de Paor, Kevin Walsh, Seán O Domhnaill particularly prominent. A bright new star was confirmed on the football constellation in the stunning performance of Michael Donnellan, the boy genius evolving into the fully developed legend, with his magnificent searing runs. Every team, to a greater or lesser extent, reflects the personality of its manager. It is no coincidence that O'Mahony's Galway represented a fascinating combination of wit and grit, of steel and style.

Prisoners of hope at first the fans from the west were both beguiled and skeptical, talking to each other to persuade themselves, listening to be persuaded that what lay before them was exhilarating - the combined intricate talents of the team fitting together in the second half like an expertly designed puzzle.

The real moment of catharsis came when Padraic Joyce smashed the ball into the net. The roar that followed was almost orchestral in its sound and feeling. After the goal Galway supporters inhaled the air, their thoughts sharpening themselves with each breath as though they had been drugged for years and were only now, with a jolt, emerging from her torpor. It wasn't just that Galway were winning. It was because they were playing the kind of slick, sweet, high-speed football that would win them new fans. A wave of euphoria washed over us and settled like a sea-mist. To fans west of the Shannon, reared on a diet of disappointment, it seemed that everything around us was heightened, emboldened, made larger than in our dreams. Lives which seemed complete enough only the night before, appeared to have gained an essential missing piece. For the previous 32 years we had known fleeting interludes of brilliance and gaiety but had reason to fear the collapse that inevitably followed, which seemed in keeping with the proper order of the universe. We had a common currency of bad memories, events replayed at different points in the continuum of time, so that our personal memories were not our own at all, but merely repetitions of each others.

This day was different and we could feel the exhilaration swimming over our bodies like a spirit making its way through a room. Banners patterned in kinetic swirls of maroon and white were proudly displayed. We will now luxuriate in the memory of that day in September, and though these memories are but echoes of the actual, they are treasures we will not willingly part with. The image of that magic moment when the final whistle sounded is imprinted upon us as is the light upon photographic paper. A protracted communal intake of breath, then a brief tighter silence still, followed by a noisy guttural exhalation. Such a state of happiness is an occasional, summer lightning thing. We know instinctively that no other sporting triumph shall ever be so dear. In an instant all the hard luck stories were washed away in the tides of history.

A day in September

September 27, 1998 was not just a victory for John O'Mahony and Galway. It was a victory for players like Mickey Kearins, Packie McGarty, Dermot Earley, Tony McManus, Harry Keegan, Johnny Hughes, Willie Joe Padden and T.J. Kilgannon who had soldiered so gallantly for so long but had missed out on the ultimate prize and a generation of Connacht football fans who had suffered and mourned in this valley of tears.

Turning-points are generally the creations of novelists and dramatists, a necessary mechanism when a narrative is reduced to a plot and a moral is distilled from a sequence of actions and the audience return home with something unforgettable to mark a character's growth. This was different, like a gift-wrapped up in deliciously pretty paper, to be given, with discretion, to the right people. Galway's victory transcended football. It was about identity and how we felt about ourselves, individually and collectively. This was a defining moment, an experience that redirected, the revealed truth by whose light all previous conclusions must be re-thought. It was a story whose historical accuracy was of less significance than the function it served, a drama that seemed to be enacted just for us.

But – hark! – some voice like thunder spake
The West's awake, the West's awake.

It was Galway's glory. But their glory reflected instantly on all of us in the West of Ireland who had so often drove home from Croke Park, sick not just from losing but from underperforming, because each of them was one of us out there and they had suddenly lifted the game to a higher plane. Sure, none of us were fit to lace Ja Fallon or Michael Donnellan's boots, but they carried us up there with them. Only five years earlier the theatre of dreams had been our torture chamber. Seventy minutes can miraculously heal a collective scar tissue.

In a perverse way it helped that we had experienced so much humiliation and disappointment in previous years. For supporters of Connacht football for most of the '80s and '90s agony was the only currency that could purchase ecstasy. If a sorcerer could magically turn pain into wealth, then all of us, would have been as rich as Bill Gates. In 1998 we finally cashed in all our misery chips.

For many of us, who had missed out on the Galway three-in-a-row in the 1960s, the desire to see our team win the Sam Maguire, was the only consistent ambition we have ever held.

An All-Ireland victory was the fulfilment of a promise of a life as it was meant to be lived for an entire province. The unthinkable had become the thinkable. The memory lingered long into the night only to be stopped gently by sleep, like a candle that been pinched out. Yet a flame had been lit that day which would fuel an entire generation. The next morning we settled into the rhythms of a new life. The haunting echoes of failure were finally banished.

The win restored the hope that sport can still be the simple, challenging life enhancement it was first meant to be. The Galway team gave football fans from the West of Ireland back our dream.

Earley to rise

Dermot Earley was having a different dream. That morning he woke early as daylight and moonlight mingled together before sunrise. Slowly, across the sky, spread a marvellous pink flush, and the trees lifted to meet it, becoming tinged with pink; and bending out into the dawn he saw the world had put on the colour and shape.

His eyes relaxed at the horizon, the place where the land meets the sky, where it appears that all movement has been suspended. Watching the sunrise, as if the world was being created afresh for him, a bubble of fresh light and colour, of brilliant sound and birdsong it was as if nature itself was feeling the wonderful rooted joy of the county he lived in. Could his young son do what he had failed to do and reach the Holy Grail?

On a normal year Earley would have shared Connacht's joy but that day was an exception: 'I am proud of all my children. I have worn the smile that only a proud father can for six baptisms, six first Holy Communions, six confirmations and each of my children have given me in their different ways many moments to be proud of.'

After his final game for Roscommon, Dermot had sought comfort in solitude: 'When I got home after playing my last match for Roscommon in 1985 I went into the garage and took my boots out of my bag. I polished them and in a small ceremony of my own, I put them up on the top shelf. I never wore those boots since. In 1987, when I was going to America to work in the UN for four years, I carefully wrapped up the boots and put them in the attic. When I came home in 1991, I checked that they were still okay and they stayed there until March 1992. I took them down one day and gave them to my eldest son, David. He wore them the day he played his first intercounty hurling game for Kildare against Dublin in the Leinster Hurling Minor League special. I was one proud man that day. I was even prouder the first time I saw David play senior football for Kildare.

'I was proud of him many, many times down the years because he played many great games for the club. I was proud the first time I saw Conor playing for Sarsfields, the many times I saw Noelle play well for Kildare and the days Paula and Anne-Marie graduated. I was very proud when my first grandchild, Oisin, was born. But it is some privilege to see your son play in an All-Ireland final. It was one of the days of our lives. You could cut the atmosphere with a knife.'

Dermot's whole face, eyes unblinking, had the look of dogged determination as he surveyed the scene in Croke Park:

'I was very proud to stand to attention for the playing of the national anthem before I played in the All-Ireland final in 1980. But there was a very special sense of pride as I stood to attention before the 1998 All-Ireland final and with all due respect to the Artane Boys Band my sole focus was on my son Dermot as he lined out for Kildare. It was incredibly emotional and it was like a surge of electricity was going through me as I felt a mixture of excitement and nervous energy.'

With the benefit of hindsight

Dermot Jnr looks back on the game with surprising detachment: 'There was a huge amount of hype in Kildare in the build-up and Galway kind of slipped in under the radar. There were posters saying: There's going to be a wedding: Sam Maguire is going to marry Lily White.

'We were three points up at half-time and I can remember thinking: we're in good place. Glenn Ryan had kept Ja Fallon quiet in the first half and in the second half it wasn't that Glenn did not play well but it was that Ja started scoring the most inspirational points, including that famous one from the sideline and, of course, they got the goal so the momentum was with them. It was only then that the country fully appreciated the great job John O'Mahony had done bringing together such a collection of great players like Michael Donnellan and giving them the freedom to play free-flowing, attacking football. They proved that they were a great team by winning a second All-Ireland in 2001.'

He modestly fails to mention that it was his own goal that had helped put Kildare in the lead. His father was less restrained in his assessment and spoke with a childlike sense of wonder: 'Dermot went one better than me when he scored a goal that day and that rose my adrenalin levels still higher. It was looking good but Galway turned on the style in the second half and Kildare couldn't live with them. Unlike our final, the '98 final will be remembered for the great skill and nobody can have any complaints the better team won.

'I was incredibly proud to see Dermot play in an All-Ireland final. Having played in the 1980 final I knew what he was going through and he handled it well. It was such a different game from our All-Ireland because both teams played such positive football. Of course, I was very disappointed for him when they lost. There had been such a feverish build-up in Kildare before the game and there was such disappointment in the county afterwards. Dermot was very young at the time and I hoped he would get another chance but from my own experience I knew that fairytales are rare enough in the GAA. As the Rolling Stones sang: "You can't always get what you want."

'I was very proud of his performance and I wanted him to know that and to try and give him a positive message as my father had done for me. There was a great sadness that my father wasn't there to share the moment. I was there that day primarily as a father and my disappointment was for my son. Fortunately, I had Mary to share the occasion with me.'

Chance rules every remote corner of the universe, except the chambers of the heart.

It was impossible not to feel the intimacy by which he spoke the name of his wife, loving what she was, her kindness, her humour, her seriousness, the goodness in her heart. She still had a beguiling almost mesmerising quality after all their years of marriage for him. It was a moment of beauty, conviction and power. Mary had a unique power to take him from the pain of the present. A flower that blooms through adversity is the most rare and beautiful of all: 'As the weeks passed, the disappointment started to fade and I became more aware of the enormity of what Galway had achieved and the style of football they played and my West of Ireland roots started to kick in and I began to bask a little in the reflected glory. It was a massive lift for the province which had known so many disappointments. I just wish they ended the famine when they weren't playing against my son's team.

'Nobody has done more than John O'Mahony to revive the football reputation of Connacht in the last generation. It was a mighty achievement for him and his team and what it made it all the better was that they did in style – playing the game the way it should be played. That Galway team showed that Gaelic football can be the beautiful game.'

A few weeks later Earley met O'Mahony: 'I congratulated him sincerely for both the win and the manner of the win. I told him he had brought pride back to the province. I meant every word I said but there was part of me that wanted to say: "Jaysus John, could you not have waited one more year?"'

There was one crumb of comfort for him in the proceedings: 'Gay Sheeran was managing Roscommon at the time and I was in touch with him fairly often during the Connacht championship. Gay did a great job with them and they came within a whisker of beating Galway in both the Connacht final and the replay. Those games brought the Galway team on a lot and I'm sure John O'Mahony would be the first to acknowledge that. If I had a fiver for the amount of times I was asked that year who I would have supported if Roscommon had played Kildare in that final I could have brought Mary on a month's holidays to the Bahamas. I was very glad for my diplomatic training for that six months.'

So who would he have supported? 'That would be have been a real emotional mess but blood is thicker than water. It would have been the best of times and the worst of times. But on the positive side no matter what would have happened it was a no lose situation. I am not sure though I would have been able to handle it but in a way I would have loved it to happen.'

When I asked him about which of his son's games for the Lilywhites had he most enjoyed, he immediately went for Saturday, August 12, 2000: 'It was the Leinster final replay. The Dubs were on fire in the first half and led by 0-11 to 0-5. Pat Spillane was writing Kildare's obituary. But 90 seconds into the second half, Dermot got a goal back and then Tadhg Fennin got an equalising goal. The pendulum swung completely in Kildare's direction and Willie McCreery was mighty in midfield. Any Kildare fan who was there that day will never forget it and Kildare ran out comfortable winners by 2-11 to 0-12. It was a great day for the Lilywhites and another proud moment for a Dad of one of the players. It was like a moment of grace, but a moment of grace that is granted only rarely.'

A family affair

Dermot was also incredibly proud of his son when he lined out for Ireland. International rules football, sometimes called 'Compromise rules' is a hybrid code of football which was developed to facilitate international representative matches between Australian rules footballers and Gaelic footballers.

The first games played were test matches between Australia and a touring Meath Gaelic football team which took place in late 1967, after Meath had won that year's All-Ireland Senior Football Championship. Following intermittent international tests between

Australia and an All-Ireland team, which began in the Centenary year of the GAA in 1984, the International Rules series really entered the popular consciousness in 1986 following a major controversy. Dermot was a supporter of the series: 'There was hullabaloo before the team went to Australia when the Dublin coach Kevin Heffernan was appointed as tour manager ahead of Mick O'Dwyer. Micko is the most successful Gaelic football coach of all time and he has never managed the International Rules team, which is extraordinary.

'However, what really made the tour come alive was when the manager of the Australian team John Todd described the touring side as "wimps" following complaints about the "excessively robust play" of the Australian players. His remarks provoked a storm of outrage not just among the Irish team but back at home at Ireland. It was a huge story throughout the country. It wasn't quite as big as Roy Keane and Mick McCarthy during Saipan but it was pretty close.

'Todd's comments were taken as a slur on the Irish character and as a result people who had no interest in the game back home in Ireland became fascinated by the series. It became a matter of national pride for us to beat the Aussies. Thankfully the fighting Irish provided the most effective rebuttal possible to Todd's comments when we won the series.

'Although people talk a lot about violence on the pitch, a lot of people love watching the games because of the physical contact. Yet the controversies the violence generated brought the games to everyone's attention and I guarantee you that when there is massive interest in the series it is because people are wondering if there will be more violence.'

Dermot watched the matches with interest: 'From my point of view it was a tremendous honour to see my son Dermot play for his country and I was delighted he got the chance to be part of the experiment to give an international outlet to Gaelic football. Of course, it did come as a shock when he was on the ball that an

Aussie player could come up and knock him to the ground by any means necessary and keep him pinned down. I do think we could learn from them. There is a very high emphasis on the basic skills but as Kerry showed in 2004 there is still a major place for "catch and kick" in Gaelic football.

'It is great for players from so called "weaker counties" in particular to get the chance to play alongside the cream of the GAA talent and to get a chance to showcase their talents to the nation. Take a player like Westmeath's Spike Fagan who could really show the country how good a player he was on live television when he played for Ireland.

'I wonder though is it possible to play a compromise game between the two codes. For example, I think asking the Australians to play a game without a tackle is like asking the Irish soccer team to play a game without heading. My brother Paul spent two years playing Australian Rules football. He went on a sporting scholarship to Melbourne, Australia in 1982 as an 18 year old having played Championship football for Roscommon earlier that year. Effectively he was a semi-professional – training and studying accountancy in college. There was a very high emphasis on the basic skills on both sides of the body because they believe that you shouldn't make elementary mistakes in a match. Here elementary mistakes are made in every match. If you were to introduce "back to basics" training sessions with senior teams in Ireland, you would be laughed at. When Paul came home he was a lot stronger because of the emphasis on weight training. His catching had improved. He was more athletic and had more endurance. The only skill he hadn't developed was his kicking because he had been using an oval ball. To my mind Anthony Tohill was the key player in Derry's success in the 1990s because of his skill and power. I suspect that he benefited enormously from his time playing in Australia.'

The Boxer

There was one time though when Dermot was not happy to see

his son wearing the green jersey as Paul witnessed at first hand: 'Dermot was irate about what happened in 2006 in the Second Test because he considered what the Aussies did was nothing less than thuggery. Many people will remember Kieran McGeeney's comments after the match: "If you wanna box, say you wanna box and we'll box. If you wanna play football, say you wanna play football and we'll play football."

'There was a dinner afterwards and Dermot was one of the guests. I was talking to one of the most high profile members of the Aussie delegation and he was trying to tell me what happened was no big deal – despite the fact that Graham Geraghty was left unconscious and required hospitalisation. I told him to stop talking through his arse.

'The atmosphere was very tense. Then Nicky Brennan, who was GAA president at the time, stood up to speak. He pointedly said before he started he wanted to wish Graham Geraghty well because he was in hospital. You could feel the tension go up another notch immediately.

'The Aussies' coach that year was Kevin Sheedy and he came over to our table and was trying to be placatory and said that it would be very different the next time and said there would be a dinner for both teams first and that would sort everything out. It was so out of character for Dermot who was always so diplomatic but he asked him: "Will you have the fight before, during or after the dinner?" Talk about an awkward silence afterwards. It showed though how furious Dermot was and I suppose the fact that his son had been playing and could have been seriously injured was a factor in his anger.'

Had he lived Dermot would also be incredibly proud to see his brother Paul manage the Irish team against Australia in 2013. Paul is now the regular analyst on Sky Sports for football games. However, in a previous incarnation he was a regular presence on *The Sunday Game*. One of his best moments came after the 1988 All-Ireland semi-final when Mayo, managed by John O'Mahony, put up a credible showing before losing to mighty Meath. At the end Michael Lyster asked Earley: 'Will Mayo be back?' Paul replied: 'I hope not!'

Managing Ireland was an experience to treasure for Paul: 'It was a great thrill for me to be made manager especially because I was working with such incredible players. Guys like Michael Murphy and Seán Cavanagh are such fantastic role models. One thing I feel strongly about is that we should market our players better. We know everything about our top rugby players but we know nothing about most of our GAA players and we should be celebrating them much more as a way to promote our games.

'At our last team meeting before we headed to Croke Park before the Second Test I asked Seán Cavanagh to say a few words about Cormac McAnallen. Seán spoke off the cuff and he was brilliant.

'I then spoke about how we all needed people to inspire us. I told the lads that two people had inspired me. One was a coach I had in Australia and the other was Dermot. I wasn't emotional and I told them about the way he always spoke about how he always felt taller and stronger when he wore the Roscommon jersey and that when they put on the green jersey they too should feel stronger and taller and go out there and give everything they had and make a difference and come off knowing they had given their very best. They were very attentive. I am not saying that was what won it for us but it was one of the pieces of the jigsaw that helped us win the series so comprehensively.'

What's the name of the game?

Watching his son's progress as an intercounty player gave Earley a keener sensitivity to the problems in Gaelic football. Ultimately Gaelic games are a spiritual experience: on a plane far higher than mere entertainment. Their liturgy is the merging of a collective spirit, the unification of minds that call every man, woman and child of a county unit at home and abroad to the altar of worship. They bring life to people and make it good to be alive. Their rituals are sacraments of the body and soul of a people - celebrations of a past that is noble, a present that is proud and a future that will be magical. Their prayers mystically invoke love of the traditions, culture and way of life associated with the faithful's home and place of origin, the club or county that nurtures a sense of belonging and identity. Their cathedrals reveal what was, is and is to come by telling us who we are and where we come from. That was why Earley was finding aspects of the modern game not to his taste:

'I am very disappointed watching some games because it seems that we had two teams who were more afraid of losing than wanting to be expressive and play the game the way it should be played.'

He had mixed feelings about the changes in the game since his retirement. While he knows its faster now he was worried that the skills are not all that they might be. Like Pat Spillane, he wanted to see the foot come back into football. He was particularly passionate about one area of the game that he felt needed to be changed:

'I do think we need to talk more about ethics in the GAA. I especially would like to see the cyncial fouls cut out. Gaelic football has such a rich tradition and we can't have that tradition scarred by the cyncisim and sometimes nothing less than thuggery that has cast a dark shadow on our games. This is not a new thing but since I have retired I have been disappointed by what some teams have been prepared to do to win an All-Ireland. I sometimes shake my head when I see some managers that I can think of feted as greats of the game when they have done so much to change the culture from playing positive football to one of stopping the opposition.

'But when I was manager of Kildare and Roscommon I was forced to reflect on my own role in terms of the instructions I was giving to the team and in particular asking for more physicality. I did not want to be responsible for sending someone out to play for me who was going to cause a serious injury. When I talked about more physicality one player would have taken that to mean to get much tighter on his man and put him under pressure when they lost the ball but maybe one of the other lads would have taken it as incitement to go out an decapitate somebody. Yes I wanted to win but no I did not want to win at all costs.'

Earley believed that teams should always be given positive messages: 'I heard Enda McNulty speaking once about studying psychology in Queens University where Seán O'Neill was a mentor of the Sigerson team. Seán was one of my all time favourite players and was a great role model for all young players like me back then because of the way he played the game – where his focus was solely on beating your opponent was through skill. That Down team he won three All-Irelands with were a breath of fresh air to Gaelic football.

'Enda recalled that he wanted to win the Sigerson more than concentrate on his studies but his greatest education as a psychologist came from men like Seán O'Neill who taught him so much about being a team payer and a leader. He illustrated this with an example of winning the Sigerson over a horribly wet weekend in Galway. Because the conditions were so bad Queens were physically drained and when they drew the final with UCD they thought they had nothing more to give but Seán was great in that situation. He told them that UCD didn't want to play extra time and were holding out for a replay. At that stage the Queens' heads lifted and suddenly were ready to go out and play extra time and they knew then there was no way they were going to be beaten.'

This was the cue for Earley to recall one of his favourite stories. In his later years John B. Keane ventured briefly into coaching. At half-time his charges were losing and were being physically intimidated. He provided a confirmation of John O'Mahony's adage: 'Whenever a team loses there's always a row at half-time but when they win it's an inspirational speech.' John

B. exhorted his side: 'Now listen lads, I'm not happy with our tackling. We're hurting them but they keep getting up.' In the second half the team showed more bite and ran out easy winners.

Suffer not the little children

There were two aspects of the modern game that were anathema to Earley: 'My big problem is at under-age level. I watch a lot of games and I wince when I hear the comments on the sidelines from coaches and parents at kids as young as seven because of the pressure they put them under and the criticism at times can be savage. I regularly confront them and ask them if they realise just the damage they are doing. Long term this sends out all the wrong messages about the way the game should be played and it helps create the wrong kind of culture and inevitably some youngsters will leave our games because they just can't stomach this level of pressure at such a young age.

'I also shudder when I see a manager who is pushing young people into situations too early - because a manager wants to win an under-21 final he plays a 15-year-old.

'We have talked a lot about burnout in rcent years but I wonder how effective it has all been. I think of a young player like Donie Shine who burst on the scene in 2006 as a minor. Everybody was clamouring to have him on the senior team, as well as the under-21 team. I'm sure it was the same for him at club level and then he was going to play Colleges football. Everybody wants a piece of him and everybody thinks their match is the most important. For a young player like that burnout is a real issue and of course there is an added risk of injuries especially with the demands on players in terms of training these days. For a young player like that it is very hard to play consistently well and often he will be asked to play when he is not fully right and then as sure as there will be showers in April there will be many fans who will start complaining about him. Seán Kilbride has a son Senan who is also a very promising footballer for Roscommon and I hope he too will be minded properly. Experience tells me though to worry for both of them.

'Another thing I see is pushing young people into a situation where they are playing with a top team and they are put up on a pedestal and then they are cut down because they don't make it and they are just cast adrift.'

The blame game

Another blot on the face of Gaelic games for Earley was a lack of respect: 'A lot of fellas have started to try and wind up opponents during the match especially if they think he can be riled up. I think that has crept in to the game in recent years. People see incidents that shouldn't happen, like in football, Paul Galvin knocking the notebook out of the referee's hand against Clare in the 2008 Munster Championship. Of course, he shouldn't have done it but people often don't realise the verbal provocation, not to mind the physical, that a player may endure. The other thing that I don't like is players diving. Think of the way Aidan O'Mahony went down after he got a little slap in the 2008 All-Ireland semi-final against Cork. That is not the Kerry way. These are two things we don't want in our games and I would like to see them addressed. I think Gaelic Games are one of the few places left where fellas are playing for the love of the game and "sledging" or trying to get a fellow player sent off are not part of our wonderful tradition and we must ensure that they are not allowed to bring discredit to our games. Players are role models. What they do young kids imitate – the good and the bad. Coaches have a big role to play in this.'

Another social problem troubled Earley: 'We in Ireland are all experts in one area: the blame game. I am not just talking about the media here but all of us in our clubs and talking in the pub we all do it. I made mistakes as a manager and I know that I have to take criticism in those situations but there has to be a line that we don't cross. When a team loses there is always a rush to judgement and some poor unfortunate the manager or the referee or the freetaker who has an off day and misses the frees who will be slaughtered to bits. Since social media has come into prominence players and managers are subject to the most savage criticism but the people responsible for these often nasty and vicous comments do not have the guts to put their names to it.'

It says in the papers

Every rose has its thorns. One of the downside of the higher profile of players has been the increased interest in their private lives with a consequent increase in rumours and malicious gossip about their off the field activities. The wife of an All-Ireland winning captain in the 1990s was sitting at home one evening when she got a call from a woman who purported to be her 'close friend'. The woman told the player's wife that her husband was at that moment in the company of another woman with whom he was supposed to be having a clandstine affair with and proceeded to describe in great detail what 'his mistress' looked like and say where they would be spending the night. The player's wife was too shocked to speak. She hung up and turned to her husband who was actually sitting beside her on the couch watching television.

Earley is concerned about the increased pressures on players and managers: 'The media spotlight has changed dramatically. There is certainly a fair bit of negativity in the media coverage. What particularly annoys me is what I consider the blight of radio phone-ins. It also creates a much more difficult environment for players and managers to operate in. You have to remember these players are amateurs but often people under the cloak of anonymity ring in and often make very personalised comments about players. We can all have a view on a pundit's comments on tv but at least they're putting their name to their comments. I don't have any time though for radio stations which give credibility to comments from a caller who has not the guts to put their name to their opinion. And of course on the internet you can say absolutely anything and sometimes these comments can be very destructive.

'Fans too have been increasing belligerent. In March 2009, Gerald McCarthy stepped down as Cork manager after receiving death threats from disgruntled supporters.

'I think we could learn a lot from rugby because of the culture they have in relation to referees in particular. In rugby, nobody dares to question the authority of the referee but that is far from the case in Gaelic games when referees are often treated with nothing short of contempt. The GAA is an incredible organisation but the one thing we need more of at all levels of our games is respect.

'I remember hearing Ireland's Olympic icon Ronnie Delany speaking one day. He said: "Respect is an enormous attribute for the younger athlete. Respect for the colours you wear, respect for your club, your county, your country, your province."'

The experience of one player in particular was deeply troubling for Earley:

'Jason Sherlock has courageously spoken of how racism has affected his life as the son of an Irish mother and a Chinese father growing up in Finglas and the difficulty in being accepted by his peers as a child because he was different, but also the racism he experienced in football both from fans and other players, and how this affected his self-esteem.

'I think the GAA should take a more active leadership role on this. We all know racism is part of Irish society and the GAA could take the bull by the horns more and try harder to stamp this out.

'I know racism is a part of a bigger issue in the GAA, sport and society, and I think education is the crucial thing. Someone like Jason is not going to get any satisfaction if someone racially abuses him and the referee hears it and suspends him because the damage is already done. It's not the punishment and the procedures, but education which is more important. We need to seriously up our game in this respect. I think the GAA is a powerful tool and they have the opprtunity to grasp the nettle and Irish society will be much the better if they do.'

The experience of the abuse that took place in Irish swimming prompted Earley to encourage the GAA to increase its measures in the area of child protection: 'My Church has been badly tainted by the scandals in child abuse. The GAA has had its own scandals in this area too though on a much smaller scale. I know from the people in charge of our juvenile coaching in Sarsfields that certainly we are trying to get our act together.'

A sad loss

Dermot believed that we have a habit of getting our priorities all wrong. We tend to confuse the most profound with the trivial and often invest minor incidents with epic importance. Treating sport as a life-and-death issue is a classic example of that.

This thought struck him on 10 March 2002 when he heard the shocking news that Roscommon footballer Ger Michael Grogan had died in a traffic accident. Dermot knew the family:

'Going to the matches for Roscommon you would always see Christy, Ger Michael's father. For Christy his son's death is still casting a long shadow over his life.

'I remember him telling me it was one of the proudest days of his life when Ger Michael came on wearing the primrose and blue jersey of Roscommon in Castlebar in the All-Ireland quarter-final against Galway in 2001.

'I remember having to struggle to fight back the tears when Christy told me the details. At about 3 a.m. his other son Chris called to his parents' house and told him that Ger Michael had been involved in an accident and he knew from the tone of his voice and his demeanour that it was serious. Ger Michael and a friend of his were returning home from the town and crashed into a wall. Ger Michael was a passenger and the driver was injured but thankfully he recovered. Nurses and doctors were doing their utmost to resuscitate Ger Michael, but it wasn't to be. The family was hoping against hope that he would recover because he was such a fine, strong lad. I will never forget Christy describing watching his son take his last breath.

'Christy was no stranger to giving bad news because of his work as a garda but hearing this traumatic tale was something else. Many's the time he had to knock on their parents' door at three, four and five in the morning. It was very sad and it left an indelible mark on his mind but I'll tell you something when it comes to hearing that news yourself it is on a whole different level of emotional devastation.'

In 2010 a monument was erected to commemorate Ger Michael. It was a moving moment for Christy and despite his failing health Dermot had hoped to be there for it:

'The memorial is only possible because of the remarkable generosity of O'Connor Monumental Works from Knockcroghery in both constructing and erecting the monument. We live in a fast-changing world and in the swirling tide of history it is easy for things and even people to be forgotten. This memorial will ensure that Ger Michael is never forgotten.

'Unfortunately many other former Roscommon footballers have died suddenly or in tragic circumstances but what singles Ger Michael's case out for me that he was the only player who I know of who died while he was a current Roscommon player. So that was the inspiration to ensure that he was remembered in this way. The monument will say of Ger Michael: "Gone too soon." No truer words were ever spoken.

'Not a days go by when his family don't think about him. There is a gap in that lives that will never, ever be filled. The heart of the GAA is respecting the past as well as the present. That is why I want to be there to pay my respects.'

It was not to be. The monument was unveiled just three weeks after Dermot's own funeral.

Fair play?

Earley believed that one of the consequences of a greater culture of respect would be a better, more transparent discipline system in the GAA. He began with reference to a celebrated episode: 'For many people the abiding memory from the 1985 semi-final between Mayo and Dublin was the infamous "John Finn incident" in which the Mayo half-back sustained a broken jaw in an off-the-field challenge.

'When you think back it says a lot about John that he continued to play on even though his jaw was broken. He was on the other side of the field from the ball when he was attacked. John never spoke about it at so it wasn't hyped up for the replay – which I don't think would have happened today. It was much later before it became common knowledge who the "culprit" was but typical of the time no action was ever taken by the GAA against the offending player.

'I am fiercely proud to be a member of the GAA but there are times I am left tearing my hair out trying to make sense of their disciplinary procedures.

'If the rules always seemed to be applied consistently it would help a lot but they don't. I think straight away of hurling and the infamous "Colin Lynch affair" in 1998. He was suspended for pulling on an opponent for two months, with devestating cost for Clare, although there was no video evidence. Yet when Michael Duignan forcefully struck a Clare player a few weeks later with the whole country watching on live television and wincing at the impact he only got a booking. That kind of inconsistency I firmly believe is damaging for the GAA as a brand and they need to try harder to get these things right. Our game is more than just a game but sometimes trying to make sense not of the rules but of the way they are implemented is like arguing with Plato in Greek.'

Earley gave two more humorous examples of the bizzare decisions that can be taken by referees: 'Mayo were playing Galway in the Connacht Championship when a player "did a job" on Kevin McStay. Kevin was badly injured and had to go off. I couldn't believe that the referee, who I knew because he was from Roscommon, wasn't booking him. I confronted him about it and he told me that the reason he didn't was that he had lost his notebook.

'John O'Mahony tells the story of a referee who was having a very strange game. He was scrupulously fair to everyone but allowed one of the midfielders on one team to run wild and to virtually decaptitate half the opposition without getting any censure. In fact he clocked up enough offences to merit eight or nine red cards but hadn't even a free given against him.

'As was his normal practice the referee had a quick review of his performance after the game with his umpires and linesmen. They said that generally he had done well but they asked him how on earth he could have allowed the midfielder to go unpunished.

'The referee calmy replied: "Well lads its very simple. It's like this. I sold that guy a tractor two weeks ago and he still hasn't paid me. Sure if I sent him off he'd never pay me."'

Raising the Banner

Earley lived by the adage that if what you did yesterday seems important, then you have not accomplished anything today. Success comes before work only in the dictionary. That is why he always wanted the GAA to do better, prising open vistas of experience and avenues of growth.

In his latter years Earley developed an unexpected admiration for Ger Loughnane. In 2006 Loughnane began an unsuccessful two years as Galway manager, where he had a jaundiced view both of some of the county's hurling officials and the training facilities:

'I was on the Hurling Development Committee, which tried to persuade Galway to come into the Leinster Championship. When we met them, one official fell asleep at the end of the table. That's a fact. Another official's only concern was that the kitchen was closing at 9 p.m., so the meeting had to be over then, so that he'd get his meal. They weren't the slightest bit interested.

'Ballinalsoe is like a sheep field. Loughrea is an absolute disgrace – a tiny, cabbage garden of a field. Athenry is the worst of all. I asked myself what were these people doing in the 1980s when they had all this success? It was Pearse Stadium they concentrated on – the stand, not the pitch. Because the pitch is like something left over from Famine times, there are so many ridges in it.'

Dermot hoped that Loughnane's comments might be the catalyst for some serious debate about the role of county boards:

'I wouldn't have put it as colourfully as Ger. In fact there is probably no topic I would put as colourfully as Ger! The GAA is a magnificent organisation. I doubt if there is any other amateur sporting body in the world to match it. I have the height of admiration for the many fine people I have met down the years who gave so much to their county board – people like the late Michael O'Callaghan in Roscommon and likewise some incredibly dedicated people in Kildare and elsewhere. That does not mean though that there are not some serious questions to be raised.

'Ger is pointing to the fact that there are many people with their own agenda and let's be honest about it for some of them, living high on Mount Ego, their main achievement is their own advancement. Local and often petty politics, egos and the desire to be in control sometimes is more important than the issues that should really be at the centre like coaching kids and developing a coherent strategy for the future to ensure that teenagers, girls as well as boys, see Gaelic games rather than sports like rugby as their natural home.

'Just take one example. Outside Roscommon and Kildare the county I would most like to see winning an All-Ireland is Mayo. People often forget that I was born in Castlebar. In 1989 John O'Mahony guided Mayo to contest a thrilling All-Ireland final against Cork. If Anthony Finnerty's kick had not gone a foot wide they would probably have won. In 1991 the Mayo County Board told John that he could not appoint his own selectors. John had no option but to resign. What happened? The next year the senior team was in disarray. There was a bad vibe all year and even though they won the Connacht final against Roscommon there was a sense in the camp that things were not going well. Probably the most memorable incident that happened in that game was that Enon Gavin broke the crossbar in Castelbar and the match had to be delayed.

'When Mayo played Donegal in the All-Ireland semi-final it was perhaps the worst game ever seen in Croke Park. The Mayo management had brought back Padraig Brogan earlier that year. Padraig had played for Donegal the previous year and when the Donegal lads saw him warming up, you could see that it gave them new energy.

'Things got ugly after that. It was probably an early example of player power. The players said that it there wasn't a change of management a lot of them would walk away. As everybody knows they spent a training session pushing cars in the Dunnes Stores car-park in Castlebar. John O'Mahony is known for his meticulous preparation and his attention to detail. Does anybody think John would have the Mayo players pushing cars in a car-park? Yet Mayo should have beaten Donegal in that semi-final and Donegal beat the hotly-fancied Dubs in the final. I don't usually do "what ifs" but I've often wondered if John was in charge that year would Mayo have won the All-Ireland?

'What did John do? He managed a Leitrim team that beat Mayo in the Connacht final in 1994. Then he went to Roscommon and woke the sleeping giant that was Saint Brigids and led them to their first county title in 28 years and set them on a journey to become a dominant force in Connacht club football. Then he went on to lead Galway to two senior All-Irelands playing football the way it should be played at its very best. I wonder if the county board officals who gave John his P45 had their own positions questioned. I could pick a myriad of other examples from other counties to cast doubt on the competence of some county boards across a whole range of issues from wrong appointments, to structures, to planning or more accurately the lack of it, to financial mismanagement.

'In the last few years we have had scandals in the Church, the banks, the medical profession, politics and business and as a result there have been many calls for accountability and transparency. County boards have huge power but who are they answerable to? I hope maybe Ger's comments could be the spark to start some serious questions in the long term interests of the Association about the role of county boards. Maybe we should get Ger to lead an audit of all county boards.

'There are some county boards that must be doing a good job. I would have to give enormous credit to the Dublin County Board for what they have done to make the county a force in hurling. This has not happened by accident but by a careful long-term strategy in the schools and clubs and with great work with development squads at underage level. I also liked the progressive thinking they showed when they appointed Pat Gilroy as the manager of their football team because they looked for someone who had experience of leadership in the business world also. It may take him a while but he is a man of substance and will do a good job. This is an example of a County Board working at its very best – but it is not always like that and sometimes not even close to that.

'The evidence suggests they are in Kilkenny for the hurlers at least. I sometimes think though that often county teams enjoy interludes of success not because of their county boards but in spite of them.'

Despite the irrepressible benignity of his nature there was one species that really frustrated Dermot:

'I don't want to generalise but I find it hard at times to stomach the minority of GAA officials who are so eager to climb the ladder that they won't do anything to rock the boat. You need people in county boards who dream big dreams and have serious moral courage not people who are terrified to offend. Those who try to be all things to all men inevitably end up being very little to very few.'

Outside forces though cast a bigger cloud on the Association.

Leaving on a jet plane

The decision of a third of the Ballyduff hurling team to emigrate in 1958 inspired John B. Keane to write the play *Many Young Men of Twenty*. The shadow of emigration lurked like a vulture hovering over its prey. It was the traditional Irish solution to economic problems. It churned out an assembly line of bodies for the boat to England and America.

Emigration was central to the culture of the west of Ireland in Earley's childhood. Communities were stripped of their young people in the same way a flock of sheep would demolish a field of fresh grass. It shaped the way people thought and felt, conditioning them to accept the grotesquely abnormal as normal. That was the way it was and that was the way it would always be. Although there were no industries there was one highly developed export, people.

There were many scenes of families travelling in block to the train station. Everyone wore their Sunday best. The mother was blind with tears. The father's eyes were dry but his heart was breaking. Men did not betray emotion. It would have been seen as a sign of weakness. The young people leaving leaned out of the window choking with sadness as they saw their parents for perhaps the last time. Younger brothers and sisters raced after the train shouting words of parting. Sometimes white handkerchiefs were produced and waved until the train went out of sight. Those handkerchiefs gave a ritual, almost sacramental, solemnity, to the goodbyes. Their presence was a symbol of defeat, a damning indictment of an economy unable to provide for its brightest and most talented.

Hundreds of young and not so young people left every year. The collective tale of woe concealed thousands of individual nightmares.

Young people wanted to stay in the country they loved but had no way of making a living. They wanted to be close to family and friends but they had no other choice but to leave. Many had good skills. Some had excellent examination results. Yet the piece of paper that was most important was the ticket to America.

We thought during the Celtic tiger that was part of our past but in Dermot's final years it returned as part of our present. The background of economic woes troubled him deeply:

'Of course the economic recession had massive repercussions for everyone but I fear particularly for the rural clubs that we are back to the bad old days again and that is a huge threat to the GAA. I have no doubt that emigration has been a major impediment to the development of football.

'Connacht counties were hit disproportionately by emigration. It is hard to quantify exactly how big an impact it has had but I have no doubt it has held back the endless stream of young footballers who left home to find a better life. What is particularly tragic is that we thought we had put all that darkness behind us but in the current recession the spectre of emigration is back to haunt us again.'

Earley was also perturbed for the future about the impact of major sociological changes in Ireland on the structure of the club.

'In rural places especially I've seen big changes insofar as the traditional loyalty to the club is weakening. There's a lot more young fellas going to third level education now and they are emigrating for the summer and playing in America or somewhere and not in their local club. I have to say I'm very worried the old style club may be in danger. The GAA will succeed and progress as long as it has the support of people; the club is the cell of growth and renewal.'

The best is yet to come

If you praise the sunshine in some parts of Ireland, you'll be told 'it'll never last'. Yet, despite the cold chill of economic recession

Earley believed that there is ample reason for optimism about the ongoing health of the GAA: 'I think there's a danger that we take them for granted. The GAA showed real leadership in revoking Rule 42 and opening up Croke Park to rugby and soccer. Nobody will ever forget the atmosphere and the sense of history in 2007 when Ireland beat England in Croke Park. It was a defining moment for many people and it meant so much to everybody in the country.

'For an amateur organisation it is a staggering achievement to have created an incredible stadium like Croke Park especially in the middle of Dublin. They have shown incredible leadership. The GAA has adapted to the changing times. They are keenly aware of the need to bringing modern marketing methods into Gaelic games. I think a critical step came in the 1990s with the decision to introduce live coverage of a large number of games on the tv. Young people get their heroes from television. If you go down to Kilkenny you will see almost every young boy with a hurley because they want to be like their heroes. In recent times you can see some young lads with hurleys walking on the streets of Dublin. You would hardly ever seen that 20 years ago. That has not happened by accident and shows the forward-thinking approach the GAA has taken.

'They have shown great creativity in the way they have managed to defy the tide and ensure that they continue to get so many people to volunteer. To me the question is: where would Ireland be without the GAA? Every Sunday and Monday morning throughout the summer especially the topic of conversation is the GAA. It just pervades Irish life. Ireland owes the GAA a great debt of gratitude. For its part the GAA owes its great players massive thanks.'

6

Simply The Best

DERMOT EARLEY was rattled. It was a rare experience for him. As a leader of men he could be counted to keep a cool head in a crisis but he never saw this coming.

In November 1993 he attended the launch of his good friend Brian Carthy's book about All-Ireland winning captains. Almost as soon as he arrived he saw the legendary Mick O'Connell striding purposefully towards him. Earley smiled his characteristic smile and extended his hand in friendship but the warmth of his greeting was not reciprocated as O'Connell said to him without any small talk: 'You said I was not tough enough going for the high ball.'

A year earlier Dermot had written in his biography when he picked his dream team:

'Mick O'Connell was probably the most skilful player that I ever saw, having the ability to do almost anything with the ball using both his feet. Of course the hallmark of his performances was his ability to field the ball high in the air.

'I came up against him for the first time in the All-Ireland semi-final of 1972. He was a legend, coming into the game following his performances for Kerry in the 1950s and 1960s. At one stage, John Kerrane, the right half-back for Roscommon passed the ball over the head of a Kerry player to me. The ball hung in the air and was an easy ball for me I had no doubt when I jumped for the ball that it was mine. But, as I jumped and my hands reached for the ball, it was not there. O'Connell, without ever touching me, or brushing against me, had won the ball. That was an extraordinary piece of skill, particularly as I did not know he was robbing the ball off me.

'His ability to drive the ball a great distance with incredible control made him almost the complete player. The only drawback that I think he had was when the games were very close and you had to use your body weight, not in any foul manner, to jostle your opponent and force your way through Mick O'Connell did not take part in that kind of football. When it did get that tight he was not involved.

'When I was a child if I was asked who I would most like to emulate when I grew up, it was Mick O'Connell. He was my hero. Micheál O'Hehir was responsible for this. He brought all these great players into your mind. The complete player to me was Mick O'Connell. The only thing I would have against him, and the reason why I do not pick him on my dream team was that, he did not have the necessary "aggressiveness", that is, the ability to fight fairly for the ball and win it, especially when the chips were down. Others might think that he more than compensated for this deficiency with all his other skills, but I feel this dimension is essential.'

The Kerry icon left Earley in no doubt that he did not agree with his analysis. Dermot was so taken aback by the intensity of his childhood idol's comments that he was unable to say anything in mitigation. As he slowly regained his composure he turned around to see Páidí Ó Sé advancing resolutely in his direction. He braced himself for another verbal attack. Páidí though greeted him effusively and then said almost in a whisper: 'You were very fair to Kerry.' He then winked impishly and walked off to the bar.

Thy Kingdom Come

Kerry had cast a long shadow over Earley's career, especially losing the 1980 All-Ireland to the kingdom. The disappointment of that match has never faded for Roscommon's star forward Tony McManus: 'I still feel aggrieved by the refereeing that day. It was outrageous. The ref was from Monaghan and I still have Monaghan people apologising to me for it. It seemed to us as if he had a preconceived idea that Kerry were destined to win and when it wasn't going according to the script that they had to get every decision their way.

'I am not one to hold a grudge but I still am annoyed by Mick O'Dwyer's reaction to it. He said nothing at the reception the next day but down in Kerry he said that dirty tactics would never beat Kerry. That still sticks in my throat. I feel they did O'Dwyer no justice. Eamonn (Tony's brother) was being denied frees despite being fouled by Jimmy Deenihan. Paudie Lynch was fouling Mick Finneran.

'There was reference made to the treatment of the late John Egan. The implication was that Harry Keegan, who marked him in the final, was a dirty player. John would have been the first to admit that Harry was not that sort of player. I think it is the only time that I ever saw Dermot Earley angry was at those comments. I felt that O'Dwyer conveniently overlooked a few tackles that our forwards had to take. Every time I went for the ball that day, I had my jersey pulled. I accept that as part and parcel of the game, but then to hear that his comments after the match you would think that all the sinning was on one side and that Kerry were above reproach. There was fouling by both teams, it was a physical game. John O'Keeffe fouled me more than anyone that year. I never had a problem with any of the Kerry lads. Myself and John O'Gara were very friendly with Oige Moran, Bomber Liston and Mikey Sheehy. All of the Roscommon players got on very well with the Kerry lads apart from Pat Spillane.'

No Pat on the Back

For his part Earley did have one altercation with Spillane. In 1979 Dermot cried openly when the Rossies beat Kerry in the national League quarter-final. After his five star performance in the All-Ireland final the previous year Spillane was widely seen as one of the greatest footballers of the time. Against Roscommon though Gerry Fitzmaurice was having one of his greatest games and was giving Spillane a torrid time. When the half-time whistle went, Earley raced up to Fitzmaurice and told him that it was he who should have been the All-Star he was playing so well. Spillane reacted badly to his intervention as Dermot recalled years later: 'I was not "sledging" Pat. I was praising Gerry to the hilt to boost his confidence and to encourage him to continue to play well. In fact it was a backhanded compliment to Pat because he was so crucial to Kerry as one of the genuine greatest players of all time I wanted to see him curtailed and Gerry was doing just that. Pat though was very indignant at my comments. In fact he was fuming. I didn't want to engage with him so I ran in to the dressing-room but he almost followed me in shouting at me that I was "only an auld fella", that I was "past it" and that I "was over the hill". I was delighted because I knew we had them rattled and that was the moment when I knew we were going to win the match.

'Pat was a whole-hearted, skillful, unselfish player for Kerry for seventeen years who thrilled crowds in Croke Park on so many occasions. He had the ability to cover the whole field. I can remember one occasion in the 1978 All-Ireland final when Kerry were temporarily without a goalie and the man who went in goal was Pat Spillane.

'He had the ability to take scores from difficult angles, mostly with his right foot. He was a quick thinker and his release of the ball was always excellent. Above all he was an inspiration to those around him. When things were going against Kerry, Spillane would be the man who would pull something special out of the bag whether it would be a catch, or a run, or a pass, or a point. It would lift the team again and establish Kerry on top.

'One of the things you would have to remember about him during his long and fruitful career was that although he had received a serious knee injury, his determination was so great that he was able to come back and perform at the highest level again, wearing that distinctive blue knee brace that everyone became familiar with. On one occasion I saw an opponent deliberately swiping at Spillane's knee with the obvious intention of re-injuring it, but nothing like that ever worked against him.

'No player on the great Kerry team bought more into the ethos that pain is temporary, glory is eternal than Pat Spillane. What can't be cured must be endured.'

Saturday Night Fever

In 2007 Earley and Spillane found themselves travelling to Roscommon for a celebrity version of questions and answers with a sporting theme with all proceeds going to the Roscommon Special Needs Association. The other panelists were Monaghan legend Nudie Hughes, Eugene McGee, John O'Mahony and former Irish rugby great Jim Glennon, who joked: 'I played rugby against Dermot Earley many years ago. He was a great player. I'm convinced though he's sent his son to replace him tonight he's still so young and fit looking.'

Thanks to the good offices of Earley's erstwhile midfield partner Marty McDermott, who played a decisive part in Roscommon's 1980 All-Ireland semi-final over Armagh in 1980, Permanent TSB sponsored the event. To add to the Roscommon football connection the event was held in the Royal Hotel run by another former Earley teammate, Larry O'Gara.

As the star guests entered the premises a young Roscommon footballer who was there to attend the famous Rockfords Night Club made a beeline for Spillane. It amused Dermot that the Roscommon player was a bit miffed when Spillane did not recognise him. The slightly humbled player sent one of his friends over a few minutes later to inform the Kerry man exactly who he was.

After the charity event was completed and the guests were making their way home they passed the young Roscommon player in the hotel corridor who was well lubricated and he made a very derogatory comment to Spillane. Having being brought up in the family pub in Templenoe, Spillane did not bat an eyelid and walked quickly past without offering any comment. Dermot though was visibly crestfallen at what he heard. Knowing that it was pointless to seek an apology, he simply shook his head at the player and walked away in silence, the glow of a great night swiftly fading: 'It should never have happened and I was mortified but fair play to Pat it was like water off a duck's back to him. Like many people he has annoyed me at times by his comments on *The Sunday Game* but I have to say he has really gone up in my estimation since he has spoken out so forcefully about the danger of young people abusing drink and also as a powerful advocate for people in rural Ireland.

'Pat grew up in the family bar and the interaction with customers from a young age sharpened his wits and prepared him for his subsequent career in the media when he has to think quickly. However, in recent times he has decided that he must speak out about what he sees as "the sickness of Saturday night Ireland" which sees so many young Irish people getting drunk, with a consequent increase in aggression and accidents.'

Earley felt that the GAA too need to confront the issue among its own members:

'Unfortunately some of our stars of the past and indeed of the present have struggled with addictions like gambling but the biggest problem has been with drink. Status can become like a drug and people are often not prepared for the end of their career. There are some terribly sad stories in the GAA. We are great at talking about some character and saying, "he was some man to drink", but then he is dead at 50. This is not good enough and we must work much harder to try and change that culture, though I know the GPA is already doing some good work in this area.'

Sponsorship was another area of concern for Earley. He was mindful of the work of Professor Joe Barry, Head of the Department of Public Health and Primary Care in Trinity College in this area which showed that participants in sport had a higher consumption of alcohol, and warns that if drinks sponsorship continues in sport then the culture of drink in Ireland will continue:

'There is no question that if induction to drinking at a young age continues, harms in later life will be inevitable and I think ultimately the GAA will be the loser. I understand the financial imperatives for the Association but we also need to be mindful to our wider obligations to society.'

Me and Jimmy Magee

In 2009 the GAA celebrated its 125th anniversary. Earley believed it was opportune to mark the extraordinary contribution the GAA has made to Irish life. The year of celebrations began with a special *Late, Late Show* devoted to the organisation. Earley was in the audience but was not invited to speak. That did not bother him. What did annoy him was that the rich contribution of the West of Ireland to both hurling and Gaelic football was barely acknowledged in the programme.

The 125th anniversary was the cue for a lengthy discussion with Dermot about his opinion of the greatest players. I told him I had failed him as his biographer by not challenging his selection of Denis Ogie Moran on his dream team. It may well have been that Ogie deserved his place on the team but I should have not let him have justified his decision on the basis of, 'one reason alone – he won eight All-Ireland medals in that position'.

I argued that he should have been selected on the basis of his talent and not the number of his medals, especially considering he played on the greatest team of all time. Dermot shrugged his shoulders and smiled and said: 'I forgive you for your failings and shortcomings.' He said though he was not for changing on this issue.

He laughed when I told him about a conversation I had with Jimmy Magee which began with 'the Memory Man' picking his dream team, then his team of greatest players of all time and to round it off, at my encouragement, his dirtiest team of all time! The contents of that latter team written on a paper napkin are safely locked in the vault of Swiss bank and will never see the light of day.

When I pointed out that Jimmy had queried the selection of Jimmy Duggan as Jack O'Shea's midfield partner on Earley's own dream team this immediate reply: 'If Jimmy had gone toe to toe with Duggan as often as I did he would have understood my selection a bit better. There were better midfielders perhaps such as Mick O'Connell and Brian Mullins but as I explained then, I wanted not the two best players but the best combination and I stand by my selection.'

For the record Earley's dream team from his playing days, excluding Roscommon players, was:

	1. Billy Morgan	
	(Cork)	
2. Enda Colleran	**3. Jack Quinn**	**4. Tom O'Hare**
(Galway)	*(Meath)*	*(Down)*
5. Páidí O'Sé	**6. Nicholas Clavin**	**7. Martin Newell**
(Kerry)	*(Offaly)*	*(Galway)*
	8. Jimmy Duggan	**9. Jack O'Shea**
	(Galway)	*(Kerry)*
10. Matt Connor	**11. Denis 'Ogie' Moran**	**12. Pat Spillane**
(Offaly)	*(Kerry)*	*(Kerry)*
13. Mike Sheehy	**14. Seán O'Neill**	**15. John Egan**
(Kerry)	*(Down)*	*(Kerry)*

If I could turn back time

Dermot had one regret about his book. For the majority of his career in the Roscommon jersey when opposing forward lines came to plunder the Roscommon goal, their invading intentions were generally thwarted by an almost invincible fortress in the shape of the massive frame of Pat Lindsay. Known affectionately to his teammates as 'the Mayor' because of his namesake Mayor

Lindsay of New York Pat was extremely unfortunate to have won only one All-Star award (in 1977) in the light of his trojan work in his defence. Pat was a giant of a man, one who tested his abilities against some of the best forwards in the game and subdued them. Dermot had one particularly happy memory of Pat: 'One day in Hyde Park, Lindsay and I were leaving the pitch, it was a particularly mucky day, the ground was heavy and we were both plastered in mud.

'As we came towards the gate someone looked at the two of us as we walked by and said to his friend: "Jaysus, would you look at the legs on them. I have bullocks at home on silage and I wish they had legs on them like that!" That was probably the most outrageous compliment we ever got in our playing days.

'At training Pat always led by example. He would do everything perfectly. His laps would never be cut short. All his push-ups were done and maybe a few extra. Everyone could see this and took great heart from it.

'In the matches we would play between backs and forwards, Pat would be marking Tony McManus. They always had great contests and there was fierce slagging afterwards. Tony would score a point. Pat would respond by saying he was trying to give Tony as much confidence as possible. Lindsay would come out and clear a ball and Tony would say something like that it was the first ball cleared out of the Roscomomn defence since 1962. This type of banter was going on all the time and it kept our spirits up.'

Throughout his career Lindsay had always togged out at Earley's right hand side in the dressing-room. On the night of his book launch the two friends shook hands and exchanged greetings but Earley felt guilty because he had not selected Lindsay on his dream Roscommon team.

When the Roscommon team of the Millennium was announced he was more pleased when Lindsay was chosen at full-back than his own selection at right-half forward.

He wanted some forum to atone for that decision. I asked him if he would consider Lindsay for selection on his greatest team of players who had never won an All-Ireland medal from his own era. His eyes lit up like a child in a sweet shop. A pen and paper was produced and the following team was chosen.

	1. Gay Sheeran	
	(Roscommon)	
2. Harry Keegan	**3. Pat Lindsay**	**4. Nudie Hughes**
(Roscommon)	*(Roscommon)*	*(Monaghan)*
5. Johnny Hughes	**6. Glenn Ryan**	**7. Danny Murray**
(Galway)	*(Kildare)*	*(Roscommon)*
8. Willie Joe Padden		**9. Joe Kernan**
(Mayo)		*(Armagh)*
10. Peter McGinnity	**11. Packy McGarty**	**12. Micheál Kearins**
(Fermanagh)	*(Leitrim)*	*(Sligo)*
13. Tony McManus	**14. Frank McGuigan**	**15. Paddy Moriarty**
(Roscommon)	*(Tyrone)*	*(Armagh)*

One player on the team was singled out for particular mention: 'Like so many players from the West of Ireland Sligo's Micheál Kearins missed out on an All-Ireland medal. Micheál Ó Muircheartaigh furnished the definitive epitaph to Kearins's career, "Some players are consistent. Some players are brilliant but Micheál Kearins was consistently brilliant."'

Update

As he was on a roll he then went on to pick a dream team of players who had emerged since his first fantasy selection in 1992.

	1. John O'Leary	
	(Dublin)	
2. Marc Ó Sé	3. Darren Fay	4. Seán Marty Lockhart
(Kerry)	*(Meath)*	*(Derry)*
5. Seamus Moynihan	6. Kieran McGeeney	7. Anthony Rainbow
(Kerry)	*(Armagh)*	*(Kildare)*
8. Darragh Ó Sé		9. Anthony Tohill
(Kerry)		*(Derry)*
10. Mickey Linden	11. Padraig Joyce	12. Michael Donnellan
(Down)	*(Galway)*	*(Galway)*
13. Colm 'Gooch' Cooper	14. Peter Canavan	15. Maurice Fitzgerald
(Kerry)	*(Tyrone)*	*(Kerry)*
	Manager: John O'Mahony	

The players unlucky to make this team were: Cormac MacAnallen, Seán Og de Paor, Glenn Ryan, Trevor Giles, Eamonn O'Hara, Ja Fallon, Johnny Doyle and Kevin Walsh.

Re-Joyce

In the language of the sport pages, greatness is common currency. In real life and in sport, greatness is a rare commodity. Greatness does not reach out its hand to the many but carefully targets a chosen few. Earley always wanted to challenge himself against the best of the best.

He was always happy to pay homage to great games, great heroes and great people. We age but memories of their magic moments and beguiling brilliance do not. The annals of the GAA have a special place for the famous players who, by their genius on the field over a period of years, have claimed a permanent place in the memory of all who love the game. It is a debt that the GAA can never repay. Every county has furnished its stars. Equally he was also keen to include some players he had often witnessed at first hand whose lack of celebrity did not diminish their profound impact on a pitch and whose commitment to the cause was no less when their side was ten points down in a league match on a windswept, soggy pitch in January as in Croke Park on a glorious summer's day:

'People think that the highlights of my career were the medals and the All-Star awards and believe me I valued each of them. But the thing I enjoyed and looked forward to the most was the contests with my immediate opponent. Because of the regularity of our battles over the years the contests I most relished were with Billy Joyce, sometimes known as "Boxcar Willie". He was a real horse of man who never took prisoners but I personally never found him to be a dirty player. I remember lining out against Galway once and was playing on a player who I considered a friend. I turned around before the throw-in and saw he had his fist clenched and he was about to punch me in the back. He turned away in embarrassment when he saw that I had spotted what he was trying to do but Billy was never that sort of player who relied on cynical tactics. I always knew I had been in a real game every time I marked him even when we won well which didn't happen too often when we played Galway.

'He was a real character of the game. Once before Galway played a big match in Croke Park, Billy took the squad by surprise by asking: "Did ye ring the airport?" His teammates didn't know what he was talking about and asked him why they would ring the airport. Billy replied: "To tell them not to have airplanes flying over Croke Park. I'm going to be jumping so high I don't want to be in collision with them."

One of their contests was particularly memorable for Earley, a day he soared through the air with the ease of an arrow: 'In the 1978 Connacht final I was playing at midfield with Marty McDermott who was a great fielder of the ball against Galway and it was an atrocious wet day. Before the throw-in Marty said to Billy: "'Tis an awful day for football." Billy looked at him and said: "You don't have to worry about it. You won't be out in it very long." He was right! Billy went in for a robust challenge, on the borders of the laws of the game, and poor Marty had to be taken off. It was a shame for him but it was one of those days everything went right for me and it was probably the only time in my career we beat Galway by a big score in a Championship match.'

With the passing years Earley relished memories of moments within matches rather than the games themselves: 'Roscommon were paying Galway in the Connacht Championship when I was tearing through the defence and heading for goal. Peter Lee came across and body-checked me and that stopped me. Micheál Ó Muircheartaigh was commentating on the match. He described the incident, "Dermot Earley is thundering through. He's stopped by Peter Lee. He's (Peter) not a big man." Then there was a pause, "But he is a broad man." I was left on the seat of my pants. When I look back now those are the things I remember rather than any statistics and of course the great friendships I made with some of my opponents like Barnes Murphy and Johnny Hughes.'

Battles of wills and wits

The other contest Earley really enjoyed was the battle of wits against the really top class players. This was a natural opportunity to ask him who was the greatest player he played against: 'Jack O'Shea, Matt Connor and Seán O'Neill would be up there but if I was to restrict it to just one it would have to be Mike Sheehy. He was a ruthlessly efficient scoring machine as I observed at first hand. A penalty was awarded to Kerry against us in the 1979 League quarter-final. I felt it was a harsh decision against us and I said to Mike as he placed the ball for the kick: "Mike, that penalty should not have been awarded to Kerry. In fair play now you should send it wide." He looked at me and smiled and then he thundered the ball into the back of the net. That was his answer.'

Sheehy would show the same assassin's certainty for years afterwards – with an attacking style so cuttingly precise as a cavalry charge of surgeons. His ability to clinically take defences apart was the product of a keen footballing brain. His approach to football seemed to borrow heavily from chess, insofar as he always seemed to be thinking three moves ahead of his opponent. Daring and dashing he was a man who was always capable of doing something stunning and he generally did: 'Gay O'Driscoll marked Mike in his first match for Kerry in Killarney when he was picked at top of the left. He never played on Gay again. Before Dublin played Kerry in a League final Kevin Heffernan went to him and reminded him about that and encouraged him to renew his acquaintance with Mike. He went in on him early in the game with a hard shoulder and knocked him over and a free was given against him. As Mike pulled himself up he said: "Ah sh*t Gay that's not your game." It completely took the wind out of Gay's sails and was a brilliant piece of psychology on his part.'

Not a man impaled on his own boasts Mike Sheehy's best moments are legendary, especially the famously cheeky free kick when he chipped Paddy Cullen during the 1978 All-Ireland final. Con Houlihan memorably described Cullen's frantic effort to keep the ball out: 'He was like a woman who smells a cake burning.'

'In his commentary Michael O'Hehir described it as: "the greatest freak of all time". Unusually O'Hehir got it wrong. It was a moment of pure genius in the speed of thought and the execution of a very difficult skill, a little parable of Sheehy's footballing genius.

'I have had a few good chats with Mike since we retired. The passage of time allowed him to look back on the biggest disappointment of his career, the defeat to Offaly in 1982 as Kerry sought an historic five-in-a row only to sensationally lose to a late

Seamus Darby goal with wry amusement. In 1982 he told me the Kerry team planned a trip to holiday to Bali in the Far East to celebrate what they had expected to be their five-in-a-row. After sensationally losing the final to Offaly one of the lads said that the only Bali they would be going to was Ballybunion!'

Up Down

Almost right to the end Earley enjoyed the company of former players. He had a particular admiration for the panache and skill of the Down teams of the '60s and '90s. They always seemed to have a treasure trove of stories. A case in point was Ross Carr.

In 1980 when Ross was just 16 he was playing senior club in one of the biggest games in the club's history and he was incredibly nervous because he had not reached the highest standards of play at all levels. His poor mother prepared a great breakfast before the match that morning but he was just pushing the bacon after the egg on the plate because he couldn't concieve of keeping it down. He got up and went to the bathroom and on the way his mother drenched him in holy water to help him play well.

He came back and this time pushed the egg after the bacon but again he could not take anything. His mother got out her rosary beads and blessed him with it. His late father was quietly reading the paper and was seemingly oblivious to his plight but eventually he peered over the paper and asked: 'What's wrong son?'

'I'm too nervous about the match to eat anything,' he answered sadly.

His father then uttered the immortal words: 'Don't worry son. You are sh*te. There's nothing you can do about that but there's no need to be hungry as well.'

Hard times

Earley also had sympathy for many of his friends when they became managers:

'Two of my former colleagues from the army Tom Carr and

John Maughan both managed Roscommon in the noughties. Tom brought new discipline to the Rossies when he became their manager. It was badly needed.'

Two Roscommon players talent for playing pool in the nude made headlines in 2002. When a second major breach of discipline occurred that summer the Roscommon County Board decided to disband the entire county panel. Given the penchant for nude pool among his senior county players Tom Mullaney, then Secretary of the Roscommon County Board, showed a flair for double entendre in his appraisal of the disciplinary measures, 'As a group all players hang together or hang separately.'

Writing in *The Irish Times*, Keith Duggan's verdict on that Roscommon policy of 'total disclosure' when playing pool made for amusing reading, 'Ah yes, the career of the Gaelic footballer can end in a flash. Just ask any of the Roscommon senior players. It will take many, many years before a Roscommon senior manager can stand before his team in the dressing-room and bellow the traditional GAA rallying cry: "Show them yez have the balls for it lads".'

In 2011 when Fergal O'Donnell stepped down as Roscommon county manager, Joe Brolly referred back to the county's former indignities with characteristic aplomb: 'Fergal O'Donnell's resignation as county manager left the people of Roscommon in shock. The big man did an excellent job. When he began his tenure, Roscommon were a laughing stock – some of their past antics made the English rugby team's dwarf-throwing look like a quiet night in over a hot cup of cocoa. Quickly, O'Donnell built them into a formidable team unit, restoring Roscommon's self-respect and reputation. His last two campaigns were excellent, bringing a Connacht title and league promotion. After a narrow loss to Mayo in the 2011 provincial final, it was clear they were a work in progress that was developing very nicely. But O'Donnell has young children. He could give no more. The problem is that the job of managing at inter-county has become all-consuming.'

Asked about this low point in Roscommon's fortunes Earley turned defence into attack: 'GAA fans in every county look to their players to inspire them, mostly for their exploits on the pitch, a rare few for their activities off it. I was really proud of two Roscommon players at that time. The first was John Tiernan. It started in February 2006 when he quit his job as a teacher and went to Guatemala, having heard reports of the devastation wreaked by Hurricane Stan in that country. He got immersed in a huge housing project. A landslide killed hundreds and uprooted thousands in that poverty-infested region. By day he built houses, by night he taught English in the local schools. Education was crucial because the whole area was locked into the monstrous barbarism of child labour.

'He would be getting on a bus to go to work and there would be kids as young as nine and ten there with little machettes going off to cut down trees to make a living. Child labour is horrific to see as I know from first hand experience myself from my work in conflict zones. John was not content to curse the darkness, he wanted to light a candle. He quickly got involved in a number of fund-raising projects like a dinner dance and sports auction. He knew that charity was not enough. His is a philosophy of a hand-up not a handout. The key was sustainable development. Accordingly, he set up an import-export jewellery business, drawing on the work of a group of widowed women in Guatemala who had formed a co-op. Having returned to teaching in Marist College in Athlone, he recruited the services of its transition year and also the transition year students in the Convent of Mercy in Roscommon to help run the business. One of the signs of his success is that his active campaigning work has made Athlone a recognised Fair-trade Town and he was part of the Athlone Fair-trade Committee on his return from Guatemala. He spent a lot of his time addressing schools and promoting Fair-trade products to try to guard against child labour and worker exploitation. John began to bring a new dimension to his development work by having the co-operative manufacture biros in the county colours of each county in Ireland and retailing them around the country. I am the proud owner of a biro in the Roscommon county colours. I was incredibly proud when I heard of his work and that kind of heroism trumps somebody playing pool in the nude.

'While he deals with serious problems I love that he also has a light side. John is a master of the funny story. Maybe one example will suffice. A well-known manager was giving a pep talk to his players about self-belief to inspire them to win the county championship. He gathered the squad around in a circle and he asks the first, Don Keane: "Don, who is the best footballer in Ireland?" Don answered, "Emmmm – Gooch Cooper?" The manager indignantly replies: "No! You gotta think that Don Keane is the best player in Ireland." Confident that this charges had learned the lesson from his master class in sporting psychology he turned to the next in line and asked: "Paul White who is the best footballer in Ireland?" He was taken aback by the response: "Don Keane?"

'I know Galway's dual star Alan Kerins is also doing phenomenal charity work in Africa. These are two remarkable players who, in their commitment to the downtrodden of the developing world, personify the best of the West.

'Karol Mannion is another Roscommon player I have great admiration for. His mother was diagnosed with breast cancer when he was 14. Thankfully she made a good recovery but that's why himself and his brother John decided to climb Kilimanjaro for the Breast Aware charity. It was really tough but they raised thousands of euro for charity. Again that is something that I took great pride in when I heard about it and those young men typify all that is good in Roscommon. They never doubt that a small group of committed people with ideas and vision can change the world. Why? It is the only thing that ever has. They live by the motto that giving in its purest form expects nothing in return.'

The siege of Ennis

Despite the manner of his departure from the Roscommon managerial job, Earley never allowed the bitter bile of resentment to invade his heart. In my final two conversations with Dermot the one player he spoke of was Seamus Hayden – who had been one of his selectors when he managed Roscommon. I asked the redoubtable Seamus why he thought Dermot never held a grudge. His answer was short and sweet: 'He was a bigger man than any of us.'

Whenever the call for help came from Roscommon, Dermot would never refuse. Loyalty to traditional allegiances was his strong point. Correction. Loyalty was his badge.

In his final years there was one jewel of memory from the sport's great theatre that outshone all others for Dermot. He lurched into nostalgia about a victory that will leave bubbles of pleasure that will never disappear.

In 2001 Fergal O'Donnell had captained Roscommon to their first Connacht title in 10 years. Dermot had been a big admirer of Fergal because of his concentration, the swift authority of his interceptions, his confident, skilful use of the ball once he had won it and above all his judgement of when he could leave some distance between himself and his marker to capitalise on an attacking opportunity and when he stayed close and uncomfortable enough to make him feel he had a hair shirt.

In 2006, when Fergal asked him to speak to the Roscommon minor team he had no sense of the epic adventure that lay in wait. His brief was simple enough to say but a harder to achieve: 'When I was asked I thought of John Evans. He first came to prominence as trainer of leading Carlow club team Eire Og. He famously said some of his team he wouldn't insult by sending them to a sports psychologist and others he wouldn't insult the sporting psychologist with by sending them to him!

'I once heard Enda McNulty speak about the need to raise our winning IQ. He explained that is what the greats of sport have. It is what makes Brian O'Driscoll so great. The bigger the occasion the more he came into his own and played not just at the top level but sets the standard for everyone else in the world. I wanted to have a bash at encouraging something like that – though I was going to use less fancy language.

'I spoke to the lads before some of their games. At one stage I spoke of the difference between a winner and a loser: When a winner makes a mistake, he says, 'I was wrong'; when a loser makes a mistake, he says, 'It wasn't my fault'.

A winner credits good luck for winning, even though it isn't good luck. A loser blames bad luck for losing even though it isn't bad luck.

A winner works harder than a loser and has more time; a loser is always too busy to do what is necessary.

A winner goes through a problem; a loser goes around it and never past it.

A winner shows he's sorry by making up for it; a loser says, 'I'm sorry,' but does the same thing the next time.

A winner knows what to fight for, and what to compromise on; a loser compromises on what he shouldn't and fights for what isn't worthwhile fighting about.

A winner says, 'I'm good, but not as good as I ought to be', a loser says, 'I'm not as bad as a lot of other people.'

A winner would rather be admired than liked, although he would prefer both; a loser would rather be liked than admired, and is even willing to pay the price of mild contempt for it.

A winner respects those who are superior to him, and tries to learn something from them; a loser resents those who are superior to him, and tries to find chinks in their armor.

A winner feels responsible for more than his job; a loser says, 'I only work here.'

'I really enjoyed the experience but I have to say that I was just a tiny part of the journey. It was the players and Fergal and his backroom team who take all the credit.'

The Roscommon minors believed him because they wanted to believe him and in Ennis claimed the All-Ireland final in replay with the inexorable directness of their running; the sureness of their finishing and in a performance where pace and positional flair were married to economy and commonsense. This boyish, thrillingly ambitious side emerged from initial nervousness to find a convincing rhythm and with the battling qualities and unfailing practicality driven in to them by their manager claimed the top prize, ending years of misery for their admirers. The icing on the cake that the team they defeated was Kerry which meant that they were less in danger of being beaten by superior talent than of being drowned in a river of adrenalin. The Kingdom were swept back as if by a landslide by the snowstorm of primrose jerseys that came exploding out of the Roscommon defence.

For the fans there was a tangible satisfaction and the celebrations that flooded the streets of Ennis with unbridled joy to wallow in their consuming love of their team.

To the very end Dermot was optimistic about the future for Roscommon football:

'When Fergal O'Donnell led the Roscommon minors to that famous All-Ireland title in 2006 he sowed a seed that will bear fruit in the next few years with the senior team. Some of those guys have a lot of potential.'

Dermot's commitment to the young footballers of Roscommon was indicative of his interest in young people in general – which found practical expression in his love for his children.

7

Love Story

THE story is about a little wave, bobbing along, having great fun. Everything is great until it notices the other waves in front of him, crashing against the shore. He is disconsolate when he realises that this is going to be his fate. Another wave comes by and notices how bad he is looking and asks, 'Why do you look so sad?' The first wave says, 'You don't understand! We're all going to crash. All of us waves are going to be nothing. This is tragic.'

The second wave says, 'No. You don't understand. You're not a wave. You're part of the ocean.'

I remembered that story in my final conversation with Dermot when he began to talk about his family. He stopped. I tilted my head, urging him to go on. He exhaled deeply. He nodded and smiled, a gentle smile, and his eyes began to moisten and a wave of sadness washed over him and suddenly, just like that, it was as if he was staring into his immediate future - like a hidden grieving that rises to grab the heart, his soul was ambushed with old emotions, and his lips began to tremble, and he was swept into the current of all that he was about to lose.

His mind crowded, as though there were a critical fact teasing him at the periphery of his brain, a detail he ought to be thinking about, a memory he ought to be seizing, a solution to a problem that seemed just beyond his grasp.

Dermot was a man capable of the most subtle investigation of aspects of the human condition, which philosophy and theology have customarily claimed as their proper territory. He felt he had come face to face with what scholastics call 'the ground of being'. Memories pricked at him, nagged at him: placing the ring on Mary's finger on their wedding day, the priest intoning the sentences with gravitas, the birth of his children. He was amazed at how intensely visceral the fear of his own death was – not for himself but for the loved ones he would leave behind. He frowned steadily, his brows knitted like a child over his homework – frustrated that area in himself had become so powerful it threatened to swallow everything else. These were his stations of the cross.

It was a tiny reminder, if one were necessary, of the absolute centrality of his family in Dermot's existence. A life is measured by the people we bring into it. By that calculation his stay on earth was very rich.

We all inhabit private world that others cannot see. A major part of living this crazy incomprehensible life is about seeing the light and humour in difficult times. Life is simply too short to be wasted on negativity. There is a limit to the amount of resolution you can muster from your own resources. When things hit rock bottom you need the example and inspiration of others to help sustain your will to fight the good fight. Dermot was fortunate in having plenty of support to draw on.

Cockiness is no crime, especially in a world where undue reticence is a recipe for being left behind, but sport is one of the areas where the penalties of overdosing on self-approval are especially severe. Given his position on the sporting ladder for decades Earley might have felt entitled to a small glow of vindication and a kind of dignified smugness.

Yet, as he told it with a waterfall of affection, the true champion in his household was not himself but his wife, Mary: 'I think back on it now and I wonder sometimes if I did neglect my family too much for the sake of my football career. There is no doubt that Mary had to shoulder the burden of bringing up our six children on her own a lot of the time and of course there were years when I was away for months at a time on peacekeeping duty.'

With his retirement from army life on the horizon he had looked forward to quietly plundering the pleasures of family life with Mary for himself.

Behind every great man

The GPO has a central place in Irish history given its association with the 1916 Rising. In the life story of Dermot Earley the GPO is of comparable pivotal importance because it was outside this building that he laid eyes on the love of his life for the first time. Dermot believed that the sporting gods were in synch with Venus because the meeting took place after an All-Ireland hurling final: 'I had been to see the game and was going into the GPO to make a phone call when three doeful looking girls caught my attention. They were wearing "Up Tipp" rosettes and were obviously extremely deflated because their native county had lost the final. I caught the eye of one of the girls and she returned my look but we passed each other without as much as a nod.

'Eight weeks later, to my astonishment, I was walking in the Curragh camp when I saw the same girl again. I sensed that she recognised me but again there was no ackowledgement on either side.

'Then we were introduced while playing badminton in the Curragh. I found out her name was Mary. I asked her if she had been the girl outside the GPO and said she was.'

As chat up lines go it was less than stellar but it achieved the desired effect: 'One thing led to another. She had a great understanding of sport and was probably the best supporter of hurling in Munster. We started to go out with one another and enjoyed one another's company. Gradually a permanent union looked right.'

It was not just her beauty alone that won Dermot: 'I would think that one of her greatest attributes is that I have never seen her flustered. I don't know if her training as a nurse has anything to do with it, but her calmness in dealing with any situation is extraordinary. It could be anything as serious as a possible crisis with one of the children, to driving the car in a tight situation. Everybody else might react and put their foot hard on the brakes and wonder when the bang was going to come but the coolness of

Mary would take us through every situation. The rest of us in the car might be numb with panic but she would always want to know what the problem was. All her family would say she was a cool customer.

'The other thing about her is that she has an immense honesty which is not always favourable to hear. Her honesty can sometimes be interpreted as criticism. When she asks for an opinion she expects the truth and when she is asked for her opinion she replies with total honesty.'

For her part Mary was quick to fall under Dermot's spell: 'I first saw him in O'Connell Street. I won't say what year! We looked at each other and when I met him sometime later in the Curragh I remembered the exchange of glances in O'Connell Street. He was certainly athletic looking and handsome too. I enjoyed his company. He had a good sense of humour and was fun to be with. All my family took an instant liking to him. He got on real well with my brother Tom. Dermot liked farming and Tom liked the help. All my family were interested in sport and because of this they already knew of him.

'Our courtship was not all disrupted by football. I was always interested in sport particularly hurling and football. As soon as I was old enough my father always took me to Munster hurling Championship games in Thurles, Cork and Limerick. Going to games with Dermot was just an extension of that.'

After a three-year romance they were married in September 1971. The invitations went out a month before the wedding.

By the time the 'big day' arrived Dermot had barely managed to control the nervous excitement within himself. His neighbour was the first to ask the question that was on everybody's lips: 'Will the weather hold?' He scratched his head as he looked up at the sky: 'By Gwad I think it will' he said cheerfully. When his wife looked doubtful he revised his opinion as he scrutinized the heavens for a second time. 'Then again it mightn't', he said anxious to cover all the options.

Their wedding reception brought its own drama. Ireland was in the middle of an ESB strike and a power cut occurred half-way through the evening. As he got ready to leave the hotel, Earley got a little bit of disconcerting advice from the Roscommon county secretary, Phil Gannon, who told him not to worry if he heard any strange noises coming from the car, someone had placed a number of stones in it and he should not be worried that the engine of his car might explode.

Hair-raising

Dermot studied P.E. for a year in London during their courtship, which was tough on both of them. Away from the discipline of army life, his hair was longer than normal so when he walked into the Roscommon dressing room Donal Keenan greeted him with the words: 'It's George Best.'

Dermot was keen to set himself in a wider tradition of Roscommon players who have had bad hair days. A case in point would be the celebrated Rasher Duignan of the great Clann na nGael club. As his career progressed his hairline receded, necessitating the application of sun cream on a scorching summer's day on his bare top. As the game unfolded Rasher was beginning to get very distressed and his performance fell well below his normal standards. During half-time in consultation with the physio it emerged that a tragic mistake had been made. It was not sun cream he had applied on his bald patch but deep heat! Undaunted the Rasher put his head under the shower and in the second half went out to have the game of his life, scoring a stunning 2-4.

For work reasons it was natural for Mary and Dermot to set up home in Kildare.

Apart from the county's strong connection with the army it is also heavily associated with racing. Given their strong farming roots the Earleys appreciated the world of the horse. They enjoyed the lore of the sport like the punter in the Curragh who bet £1000 on the winner of the first race at 15/1. When he went to collect, the bookie told him he didn't have £15,000 in the bag. Could he drop back a few races later? He did, and the bookie, who was losing all round, still did not have enough cash. Would he take a cheque? 'No, I bet cash and I want to be paid in cash,' he snapped. 'And if you're going to be running me around like this, I'd just as soon call the bet off!'

All you need is love

Marriage is like a bicycle made for two when at different times one partner has to pedal harder than the other. Mary would help Dermot through his darkest moments.

On his second peace-keeping mission abroad, she joined him for a two week holiday in Cyprus in 1983. His father and mother would look after the children in Newbridge for the fortnight, Mary brought over a tape with a recorded message from Peadar Earley. The tape was listened to and carefully stored away and played for only the second time in May 1992.

Listening to his father's tape was emotionally draining. The words were not spoken but gasped. His father's obvious struggle to breathe cut like a knife. While his lungs were clearly failing his brain was still razor-sharp. He provided an up-to-date account of local and national news and provided an informed opinion about events in the Middle East. He gave an assurance that his health was on the mend. The words said one thing. The breathing gave a very different message. There was a long silence between us when the tape was over.

On 24 February, Earley took his wife out to dinner to celebrate his 35th birthday. There was a note waiting for him when he got back, telling him to report urgently to HQ. Despite the high temperatures he felt chilled to the bone. He knew intuitively that it was bad news about his father. The previous night following a bad turn, his father was admitted to Naas hospital:

'As soon as I returned to Ireland I headed straight to the

morgue. I never saw my father looking so good. You never understand what death is like until it comes close to you. You hear about the coldness of death but it only struck me when I touched him on the forehead.

'I will never forget the burial. The funeral Mass had to be held in the parish church because the local church would not be big enough to hold the crowds. The funeral had to pass the house and the school. The hearse stopped outside the school and the coffin was taken out and carried the mile to the graveyard. I was calm and in control of the sorrow within me until we stopped outside the school. This was the hardest moment of all. Mary understood what was happening and told me: "You have been very good up to now. Keep control". The moment passed and that is the single moment I remember clearly.

'When I look back now every time I had a wobble, Mary was the one to tell me what I needed to hear and get me through the hard times like that one. For 40 years now she has been the light of my life as well as the love of my life.'

When infatuation had worn away her husband's footballing exploits gave Mary a whole new insight into the "Monday morning wash":

'Thank God for the washing machine but grass stains on white togs were always a problem.'

She was to reap unexpected rewards though from her husband's fame: 'Dermot was often asked to give talks. Once he went to Clonown (a small town on the Roscommon side of Athlone). At the time Brendan Shine had a very popular record out called "Carrots from Clonown". As the talk finished a man walked up to Dermot with a big sack on his back and said: "Here's a few carrots from Clonown." We didn't need to buy any carrots for the next two months.'

When two become one
From the outside the Earleys seemed an old fashioned couple. The

husband was expected to be head of the family, on whom responsibility for its survival depended, the provider, who made all the key decisions. The wife owed, not obedience, but acceptance of his decisions. She stayed at home, had the children, looked after them and ran the house. The father was the custodian of order, the mother was the catalyst of love and warmth. Yet this was a totally misleading picture. Far from being a hierarchical relationship their relationship was egalitarian. They constantly consulted one another, shared decision-making and accepted an equality of worth.

Such was the intimacy of the relationship and their shared desire to know and be known, understand and be understood, express and receive feelings at all times that more often than not their six children thought of them as one unit. They appeared to have found the perfect balance between closeness and separateness, similar and dissimilar views, dependence and independence. They constantly affirmed each other's strengths and abilities. Their greatest gift was empathy. They knew intuitively each other's fears, anxieties, insecurities and moods. Neither was afraid of the vulnerability that loving entails because they recognised that without love, we are birds with broken wings.

I once jokingly asked Mary, in Dermot's presence, if she was ever sorry she had not married a Tipperary farmer. She replied: 'Maybe if he was a county hurler!'

Thankfully God gave us the imagination to compensate us for what we are not and a sense of humour to console us for what we are. D.I.Y. was an interest of Dermot. Although he set about the task of redecorating his house with gusto there was a significant discrepancy between his enthusiasm for the task and his ability to perform it successfully:

'Mary always said that if she had to pay me by the hour she would be broke along ago.'

Mary would introduce him to not one but two new loves. The

first takes us, at heart, into a mythic place, an ageless space alight with Celtic warriors – not men but Giants – who know who they were, are and will be. It is not just part of who we are – it could be argued it is who we are:

'Before I met Mary I enjoyed hurling but she brought my interest in the game to a whole new level. Hurling is woven into Irish history. The roar of the crowds, the whirr of the flying sliotar and the unmistakable and unique sound of the ash against ash has enthralled sport fans for decades. Mary showed me that nothing captures the unique magic and tribalism of the GAA more vividly than a Munster final. To see it at first hand was to know that the GAA is about more than sport: it is about identity and pride in one's place – something bigger than just the players on the pitch, it feeds into an evolving tradition that belongs to greats of the past and to the heroes of tomorrow.'

Although Dermot brimmed with contentment and connection of the place and people he loved in Roscommon the other thing he got from Mary was a deep admiration for a new county with its country air sweet with the scents of the ripening meadows: 'I think the first lesson I ever learned from Mary was that God is everywhere but he spends most of his time in Tipperary!'

The sweetest feeling

Although he had a reputation for clean-living Dermot did have one vice. His son Dermot acknowledges: 'Dad had a fierce sweet tooth. Mam is still finding out to this day about different times some of the six of us would have gone off somewhere with him in the car with strict instructions from her about not spoiling our dinner by eating something. Every time we were in the car Dad would ask: "Will we stop for an ice-cream?" We always knew the answer was going to be yes but we would never let on to Mam.'

One of the qualities that made Dermot a happy man was his ability to take great pleasure from the simple things in life. Outside his love of his family and the joy of wearing the primrose and blue of Roscommon for the first time in all our conversations over 20 years the incident I heard him speaking most effusively about was pleasure going to attend a training-session at Saint Brigids' club with his former teammate with Roscommon, Seamus McHugh:

'I had the biggest steak I ever had in my life afterwards in his house. I don't think I have ever tasted anything as good. Nothing has ever given me more pleasure.'

Dermot was fiercely proud of all of his children. He glowed as if he is transmitting electricity while he recalled the lineage of love and his first memory of Conor in the hospital: 'Mary proudly showed off our new treasure to me. I had often visited people in hospital but a maternity ward was a different world, a palace of tenderness and chaos. Studying Conor's new face was incredibly exhilarating. We marvelled at his tiny, chubby face, with his constantly changing expressions, his miniscule hands and fingers swinging around like a bicycle wheel and his round, demanding tummy.

'Paula's sympathetic and understanding nature make her an appropriate person to follow her mother into the world of nursing and I am proud that the family tradition in the caring professions is being continued.

'I was delighted when Anne-Marie decided to become a teacher. In a way I felt she was keeping on the family tradition from my father. She knows how highly I value the profession and how pivotal I believe a teacher can impact on the life of a young person. She is acutely aware of how my father influenced me as a teacher. There is one story I have often told her.

'For me there were advantages and disadvantages in having my father as my teacher. The advantages were that I could call him whenever I needed assistance with homework or required points of clarification. The disadvantages were that I could never skip on homework or use the classic excuse: "Please Sir I forgot my copy." There was one time that I realised that my father often saw more than he let on at home.

'We were given particularly difficult sums involving addition, subtraction, multiplication, and division. If you made a mistake in the beginning you got the whole thing wrong. My father was watching me that night but did not make any comment. The next day he was correcting the sums when he asked all those who got them right to put up their hands. I put up my hand. He walked down and asked: "Is that the answer on the board?" I said no. He said nothing more until later that evening. All the lads were gathering outside to play football. I was all set to go out to play with them but my father said: "Come here you. Where are you going?" "Out to play football." "No you are not. You told me a lie today. You are staying in all evening."

'He never said anything else. I stood at the window watching the lads going to the match. It was the longest two hours that I ever spent. I will never forget it. It taught me a lesson. Never tell a lie. We often talked about it afterwards. When I had kids of my own and was chastising them for telling lies he would say: "Your Daddy will tell you all about telling lies." It was the right way to do it. It extracted the maximum punishment and he never laid a finger on me.

'If Anne-Marie can have even a fraction of the influence on some of her pupils that my father exerted on me she will have the type of fulfilling career that I wish for her.'

At the height of his football career one of Dermot's children would unwittingly embroil him in controversy: 'In 1980 as we left our Dublin hotel before the All-Ireland semi-final against Armagh David, who was four and a half at the time, was togged out in his Roscommon's outfit and by my side. David was part of all our build-up and saw himself as an unofficial sub on the team. It had been patiently and painstakingly explained to him that he would accompany the team to the hotel but would then travel separately with his mother to the match. When the point of separation came David went into hysterics. After all efforts at placating him had failed I reluctantly allowed him to travel with the team.

'David was watching the teams getting ready for the parade from the dugout when Danny Burke urged him to join me on the pitch. This caught me by surprise but I had no option other than to take him by the hand and parade with him.

'As Roscommon already had a mascot there was controversy after the match about the incident. A press report referred to the "immaturity" of Roscommon for allowing the situation to arise. GAA headquarters issued a directive before the All-Ireland final saying that no mascots would be allowed for the big game.

'After the Armagh match the Roscommon fans were so ecstatic that David became frightened as he was engulfed by a sea of blue and yellow when Roscommon fans invaded the pitch. Having successfully retrieved and consoled him, I was then able to savour the joy of winning.'

History makers

Good habits are learned young. As a boy legendary cricketer Brian Lara learned to bat using a scrunched-up evaporated milk can as the ball. If he missed it, it cut his leg. He didn't miss very often.

Scientists have never unravelled the nature-nurture question, whether talent is inherited or can be instilled. Bill Shankly, the sage of Anfield, had no doubts, 'Coaches don't make great players, mothers and fathers do.' Tony Blair famously said, 'At this stage I value judgement more than intellect.' In Kerry parlance an ounce of breeding is worth a ton of feeding. The Earley children were to keep the family name in lights because of their achievements on the sporting fields:

'Noelle was born in 1984, the GAA's Centenary year. When people asked me how many children I had I would always say: five and one for Centenary year.'

Although he had scant interest in statistics or personal milestones as the years passed and records came his way, it became increasingly hard for others to ignore them: 'I was so proud to see Noelle become a top class ladies footballer. So it was such an honour for the family when Noelle picked up an All-Star award in the City West Hotel in 2009. She was only the second Kildare woman to win an All-Star. She was at the top of her game so it was a fitting honour for her. I was delighted for her and because I knew she appreciated our special history with the All-Star awards. The same year Dermot won an All-Star and they were the first ever brother and sister to win All-Stars in the same year. It was nice for me because Noelle helped me make history because no father, daughter and son had won these awards before. I'm not sure if Noelle was the first person to win an award whose uncle was also a winner because Paul won one in 1985. Knowing Noelle was getting an award trumped my own joy when I won my own two awards.'

The final curtain

The six Earley children were aware of their father's footballing pedigree from an early age as Dermot Jnr acknowledges: 'A very vivid memory for me was Dad's last game for Roscommon against Mayo in the 1985 Connacht final. After the game was over myself and my brother Conor ran across the pitch on Hyde Park and he embraced us. I remember how dejected he was when he did an interview afterwards with Jimmy Magee. I also clearly remember when they beat Galway in the semi-final because he had his jaw broken in that game. When he came off people thought it might be his last game so they were all standing and clapping.'

'Roscommon went into the Connacht final as firm favourites having beaten Galway in the semi-final playing what was described in the media as "champagne football".

'Playing corner-back for Mayo that day was Dermot Flanagan, who exactly 20 years earlier Dad had once babysat in Ballaghadreen.

'In his victory speech the Mayo captain Henry Gavin paid tribute to Dad but just as at that point the microphone went dead.

Henry continued to speak, not realising that the Public Address was dead. Nobody heard what he had to say. There were remarks of kindness and good wishes for Dad's retirement. Dad could not help but see the irony – he lost a game the team had been expected to win, it was his final match and then, at the precise moment when Henry was about to offer complimentary words, the microphone went dead.

'Apart from losing the game Dad's other big regret was that because he was delayed doing an emotional radio interview with Jimmy Magee when he confirmed that he had played his last game for Roscommon and spoke with a number of well-wishers he missed out on Pat Lindsay's announcement that he was retiring. By the time Dad returned all the players had left and he was bitterly disappointed to miss out on Pat's characteristically rousing speech.

'In anticipation of victory the Roscommon County Board had champagne in the dressing room. It was the only time Dad ever had champagne after a match. It tasted a little flat and was a metaphor for his mood.

'The following Saturday morning the radio was on and as the family prepared to have breakfast we were surprised to hear the late Treasa Davidson say on the *Playback* programme: "And then there was the Connacht final and Jimmy Magee's interview with Dermot Earley." We could hear the lump in his throat and the emotion in his voice as Jimmy asked him: "Is it all over?"

Dad responded: "It's all over. There's no going back now Jimmy."

"Now that is over that will you miss?" Dad replied: "Well, I will miss the training and the camaraderie, the run from the dressing-room and the roar from the crowd." There was silence and Jimmy came back and said: "The last five minutes have been pretty hard." Dad answered: "Pretty tough Jimmy." Then it was over. Treasa Davidson wrapped up by saying: "Jimmy Magee and a doleful Dermot Earley."'

Pain in the ass

Like his father before him Dermot has now started to dip his toes into media punditry. His father's favourite pundit was Anthony Tohill because he believed the big man always chose analysis over entertainment.

Into every pundit's life some rain must fall. Dermot was a big believer in the moral of the GAA analyst, the donkey and the bridge. A man and his son were bringing their donkey to the fair. The man was walking with the donkey and his son was up on the animal's back. A passer-by said: 'Isn't it a disgrace to see that poor man walking and the young fella up on the donkey having an easy time. He should walk and let his poor father have a rest.'

So the boy dismounted and the father took his place. A mile later they met another man who said: 'Isn't it a disgrace to have that boy walking while his father takes it easy. You should both get up on the donkey's back.'

They duly did but a short time later they met an enraged woman who screamed: 'How cruel it is to have two healthy men up on that poor donkey's back. The two of you should get down and carry the donkey.' Again they did as they were told but the donkey fell, as they walked over the bridge, into the river and drowned.

The moral is that if you are an analyst and you are trying to please everyone you might as well kiss your ass goodbye.

As in so many other areas Dermot Jnr has learned from his father's wisdom:

'He always taught me to be my own man. It's a very important part of being a pundit. It's also very important for me in my army career.'

8

An Officer And A Gentleman

THE anthem for the Sixties generation was 'Hope I d-die before I get old'. Theirs was the era that saw an unprecedented departure from previous epochs. It was in the Sixties that life as we know it today was shaped and moulded. It was the decade of the Beatles, pirate radio, monster peace-concerts, flower power and Mary Quant. Hope and idealism were the common currency. Nostalgically everything about the time seems good, the concern for peace, the socially concerned songs of Bob Dylan and Joan Baez and the sense of freedom and optimism.

Higher educational standards, greater foreign travel and industrialisation opened the windows of change on Irish society. However, the greatest agent of social transformation was unquestionably the emergence of television when topics, which had hitherto being shrouded in a veil of secrecy, were openly discussed for the first time in pubs and parlours.

Ireland had now entered the era of the global village. At the flick of a switch the world was at the viewer's fingertips. No picture was more dramatic than the sight of Neil Armstrong walking on the moon on 1969 and uttering the immortal words: 'A small step for man and a giant step for mankind.'

The deep silence of the Irish countryside swallowed up the music of change hungrily. It was a time to dream and every dream seemed achievable.

JFK

For the young Dermot Earley one man's high hopes typified the mood of change that was sweeping the nation:

'In 1963 when I was still in school John F. Kennedy came to visit Ireland. The aspect of the visit, which I noticed most, was the time the army cadets formed a guard of honour in his presence. The glamour of the occasion appealed enormously to a young lad who was thirsty for adventure and excitement. This appeal was accentuated when the Irish government received a request from America for the cadets to be present at President's funeral at Arlington, which the government acceded to. The eyes of Ireland and the world were on the funeral, and there in the midst of all that attention were the Irish cadets. If any proof was needed that life in the cadets would produce drama and stimulation, this was it. I never had any regrets – though I would have loved the opportunity to study medicine because of the potential to help people.'

Lieutenant Late

Dermot's army career would afford him many opportunities outside the professional realm. Although he might never have had the career of Brian O'Driscoll it nonetheless comes as a shock to discover that Earley turned down the opportunity to play international rugby: 'I had never even seen a rugby ball till I joined the army but I really enjoyed the game and got the chance to play against some great players like Mick Quinn who went on to have a distinguished career with Ireland and Leo Galvin the only Roscommon man to play rugby for Ireland.'

While on army duty in the Middle East he took the opportunity to play rugby with a side called 'The Wild Geese' who were comprised of Irish army exiles in the Middle East. In matches against the top club sides Earley made such an impression that he was invited to become an Israeli International! Politically this was out of the question.

Dermot's sense of history made him uncomfortable with the fact that Ireland's first president and fellow Roscommon man, Douglas Hyde, was removed as a patron of the GAA within a few months of his inauguration in 1938. This was because Hyde had the temerity to attend a soccer game between Ireland and Poland at Dalymount Park and in the process, breached the GAA's ban on foreign games. In effect the GAA had a vigilante committee whose brief was to attend 'foreign games' and report GAA members in attendance either in a playing or supporting capacity.

In 1887 one of the GAA's founding fathers Maurice Davin had called for a ban on rugby and soccer. The political leanings of the GAA had been clearly manifested in 1902 when Rule 27 'The Ban' was introduced. It prohibited members of the GAA from playing, attending or promoting 'foreign games' like soccer, rugby, hockey and cricket. The ban was clearly shown to be out of step with the times in 1963 when Waterford hurler Tom Cheasty was banned for attending a dance sponsored by his local soccer club. The ban cost him a National League medal.

When Earley played for the army it would have been folly for him to be seen playing rugby from a GAA perspective. As a result the team could only have 14 players in the team photograph. Sometimes the referee might stand in for him. This became something of a recurring joke in rugby circles. On one occasion a referee walking on to the field said: 'Let's get the photograph over, because I know I have to stand in here for your man.' The press officer of the rugby team came up with an assumed name for Dermot – Lieutenant Earley became Lieutenant Late.

The bare necessity

While Dermot enjoyed the sporting element of army life some of the disciplinary measures were a little less fun: 'It was a different army then in many ways. I got my hair cut before I joined in October 1965. On my first day I got a pat on my shoulder and was told to get my haircut again – which I did. Three hours later I was pulled aside by another army officer and sent for a further haircut.

'One day there was a room inspection. I had gathered all the rubbish that I needed to dispose of it, but I had forgotten to actually dump it. To my horror I discovered it just before my room was due for inspection. Thinking quickly, I put the dustbin into my duffel bag, which I used to carry my football gear. Then I threw the bag out the back window, which faced on to the public road. Seconds later the inspection began. Everything was going beautifully until a little lad came bursting in the door carrying the bag in his hands saying: "Is this yours, mister?" As you can imagine this caused a little bit of difficulty.

'Another day I was in my room getting ready for an inspection in the square. It was one of those formal events where everything had to be absolutely perfect. Before I went out for parade I checked myself in the mirror. With my shoulders square, my chest out and my rifle on my back, I must confess that I thought I looked pretty good. Unfortunately, as I turned around and put my gun on the shoulder, the rifle hit an almighty wallop on the lampshade, shattering both the shade and the bulb to pieces. Pressed for time, I brushed myself off and disposed of the evidence under the bed. As I stood stiffly waiting for an inspection the Officer-in-Charge walked behind me only to return with a large piece of lampshade. He was curious to know what piece of new equipment I was introducing to army life. As I was going redder than beetroot with embarrassment, my colleagues were trying vainly not to breach military etiquette by bursting into laughter during inspection time.

'One of the tasks I was given was to dig the grass off the tarmacadam with a spoon to ascertain if I would obey orders without question. I did.'

There was one other priority for Dermot once he joined the army: 'My father's parents died when he was very young. He told me that he gave his first wages as a teacher to the man who brought him up. I never forgot that story. When I entered the cadet school I got a cheque for £4 in my first week in the army. I cashed the cheque and sent the four crisp pound notes to my father. He never said anything about it but he put the notes into his wallet and they were still there when we went through his personal effects after he died in 1983.'

In the army now

Having joined the Defence Forces as a cadet in 1965 Earley was commissioned into the Infantry Corps in 1967 and appointed a Platoon Commander in the Recruit Training Depot at the Curragh. He specialised in Physical Training and Education and was appointed an instructor at the Army School of Physical Culture in 1969. He then went on to Strawberry Hill College in London for a year to study P.E. He was awarded a distinction and got first place in his group. An integral component of the college year was teaching practice. He made the trek for his teaching practice to a part of Slough with the memorable name of Shaggy Calf Lane.

One of 10 other students from Ireland on the course was Cork goalkeeper Billy Morgan who had two abiding memories of Earley's time in London: 'I remember there was a lot of talk in college, about his abilities as a rugby player, particularly after one match. The college team got a penalty in their own half of the field. The captain was shaping up to take it when Dermot asked if he could have a shot at the goal and he calmly slotted it between the posts. The talk among those in the know was that he was good enough to become a full international for Ireland, if he concentrated all his energies on rugby. I am told he was an excellent goalie and could have made it at soccer too. He was a great all-rounder.

'A significant part of our studies was the writing of a thesis. We had to present a summary of our argument to the class. I did mine on Gaelic football. My essential point was that our tactics were too stagnant and that some innovation would improve the game. I stressed particularly the benefits of introducing a third man mid-fielder into the game. One member of the group objected vehemently to my suggestions and the others rowed in with him. The only man who spoke out in favour of my proposals was Dermot. He saw a lot of merit in the ideas I advocated.'

Earley and Morgan won the first All-Ireland sevens together and the respect went both ways: 'Billy was as good a goalkeeper as we've ever seen. Actually he is the best I have ever seen. He had this mighty leap off the ground and was the archetypal safe pair of hands. In those days you'd forwards and backs all coming in on top of him and Billy would come out on top of everything and soar through the air through the melee and grab the ball or at least punch it to safety. He had great guts. He was scared of nothing and would go in where no sane person would to protect the goal. The best thing though was that he had the sharpest eye I've ever seen which left him with such great anticipation that he could make a really difficult save look very easy.'

A Man's Life

On Earley's return home he found himself in the limelight: 'I was one of a group of army personnel who worked on an advertisement for television that would encourage young men to join the army. The group did lots of physical activities like abseiling down a cliff and "sang":

We are rangers, mighty, mighty rangers

We can do it. We can make it.

The advertisement closed with the phrase: "The army: it's a man's life for you." The advertisement won an award in a major European competition for "ad of the year".'

As diligence, meticulous preparation and minute attention to detail were the cobbles on the road on which he travelled Dermot was a natural fit for army life. He told the story about the four most powerful people in life namely: Everybody, Somebody, Anybody, and Nobody.

There was an important job to be done and Everybody was sure Somebody would do it.

Anybody could have done it, but Nobody did it.

Somebody got angry about that, because it was Everybody's job.

Everybody thought Anybody could do it, but Nobody realised that Everybody wouldn't do it.

It ended up that Everybody blamed Somebody but Nobody did what Anybody could have.

The great thing about the army for Earley was that everybody knew exactly what they had to do. His philosophy was the minimum of fuss and the maximum of efficiency.

Moving up the ranks

Over the following years he held a variety of operational and administrative appointments in the Curragh Command and completed the First Ranger Course in the Defence Forces, which led to the establishment of special operations training and the formation of the Army Ranger Wing. Following a period as Assistant Command Adjutant at Curragh Command Headquarters he was appointed School Commandant of the Army School of Physical Culture. From 1983 to 1987 he was desk officer for overseas operations and later current operations in the Chief of Staff's Branch at Defence Forces Headquarters. He would later serve as an instructor at the Command & Staff School of the Military College and help establish the United Nations Training School Ireland in the Military College.

There were some light moments along the way. Traditionally the army had a mission every Lent. In 1979 Fr Michael Cleary gave the mission. In one of his talks he spoke about determination and compared determination with Dermot Earley going through with the ball for the goal, much to the amusement of the rest of the congregation. On that Ash Wednesday Earley was going up to receive the ashes when Fr Cleary revised his blessing somewhat. Instead of: 'Remember man thou art but dust and into dust thou shalt return,' - his blessing was: 'Up the Dubs.'

Throughout these years Earley built up some great friendships in the army through playing football for the army team. One of them was with former Dublin star Tommy Carr: 'The one word I always associate with Dermot is respect. In any role in the army he had whether in work or on the team the thing he commanded was respect. He never demanded it but earned it because of who he was as a man. The other reason I admired him and I am sure I am not alone this is that he always showed respect to everyone he met in the army and beyond.'

Déjà vu

Dermot possessed all the necessary leadership qualities to succeed in the most high-pressure business of them all. However, one thing that set him apart was that he was a brilliant public speaker. Micheál Ó Muircheartaigh said of his speeches: 'You'd sit back and listen to him and hope it would go on a little bit longer.'

Whenever he spoke in public he invariably told a joke against himself. He turned self-deprecation into an art form.

His favourite was that one night he was approaching Roscommon town when he saw a teenager thumbing a lift. As it was raining he picked him up. As they got close to the football pitch Dermot asked the youngster if he had ever played in Dr Hyde Park. The young man replied: 'Many times.'

Dermot said: 'I played a few good games here myself. In 1973 Roscommon were playing the All-Ireland champions of the time, Cork here. The team were just a point ahead in the last minute when Cork mounted an attack and I made the saving clearance.'

The teenager replied: 'I know.'

Dermot continued: 'In 1977 I played on with a broken finger and helped Roscommon beat Galway in the Connacht final.'

Again the young man responded: 'I know.'

Undeterred Dermot persisted: 'I once kicked a 50 against a gale force wind and landed it over the bar in a match against Down.'

Yet again the young man's reply was: 'I know.'

By now Dermot was puzzled and asked his companion what age he was. When his guest replied that he was only sixteen Dermot asked: 'All those matches were over 20 years ago, before you were even born. How could you possibly know about them?'

The teenager sighed deeply before saying: 'You gave me a lift two weeks ago and you told me the exact same things then.'

David Earley provides another example of that genre:

'Dad often spoke about meeting an old man from Roscommon who told him that he had seen all of the times he played for the county senior team. He recalled each of Dad's great games and how brilliant Dad had been in it. With each game Dad could feel his chest swelling bigger and bigger with pride. He was beginning to think he was the greatest thing since the slice pan. Then the old man finished off: "Ah, you were a great player and you kicked great scores – but you could kick a lot of wides as well!"'

Despite his intense love for Roscommon, Dermot was not above poking some gentle fun at the Rossies. He liked to play the game: what country would a county be based on its GAA team? He said that Meath would be Al Queada because they took no prisoners. Roscommon would be Japan – their last great campaign was in the 1940s.

One former army colleague who saw the impact of Earley's speaking skills up close and personal was Kevin McStay: 'In 2008 I got a fantastic appointment with the Irish component in Kosovo. I was there as group logistics officer. It was like being the manager of a 200 bed cheap and cheerful hotel. I was there if or seven months through a dreadfully cold winter where the weather could go down to minus 15 or minus 25 so I had to try and make sure that everyone had a reasonable standard of living and ensure that over 200 army personnel were fed three times a day. We were very well looked after. It was one of the most challenging tasks I ever took on but incredibly rewarding.

'It also brought home in a very striking way the importance of peacekeeping for me. I remember going to a village where there was a massive graveyard where 40 or 50 people had been killed on the one day in a massacre. Each grave had a little cross and each had the same date. They also have the ages of the deceased from old men to young children. It was incredibly poignant and sad and underlined the necessity for our work there.

'On that trip I had a big responsibility for the visit of the Chief of Staff and of course it was Dermot Earley at the time. He was the most amazing man I met in the army. I played with him for the army team. I played against him in the 1985 Connacht final. He was just an incredible human being with unbelievable standards as a man, a footballer, as a leader and as an army officer.

'On that trip Dermot spoke for an hour to the troops in a big hall. Some of them would have had very little contact with him before that and the younger ones in particular would have been aware that he was Chief of Staff but not much else because you can be in your own bubble a lot when you are in the Defence Forces.

'His theme was that while they were there they would make hundreds of decisions and the vast majority of them would be right because that was the way they had been trained. However, there might be times when they would make wrong decisions but that if they made wrong decisions he would understand and be sympathetic if their intentions were good. It was a very encouraging message to give everyone.

'By the end of the speech though they were all in awe of him and they all wanted to shake his hand and get photos taken with him. He just had that special talent to speak to a big group and enthuse everyone and then make everyone feel that they were valued when he spoke to them individually. It was just a great insight into the nature of leadership to observe him in action and the way he used his position to give every one a sense that although they were away from home and missing their families he really appreciated what they were doing and that they were making a real difference to serving the cause of peace in this troubled region.

'It was just a privilege to see him at work close to hand. You would never meet Dermot without him leaving an impression on you. It's such a sad time now that he's left us.'

Top gun

Dermot's army career saw him taking up many different roles. In 1995 he was promoted to Lieutenant Colonel and commanded the 27th Infantry Battalion on the border with Northern Ireland. He was promoted to Colonel in 2001 and was the Director of Administration and Director of Personnel before being selected for promotion to Brigadier General in 2003. He was promoted to Major General in 2004 and was appointed Deputy Chief of Staff. All the while he was furthering his education with a Master of Arts in peace and development studies from the University of Limerick.

In June 2007 he became Chief of the Staff of the Irish Defence Forces. He had an almost evangelical conviction in his voice as he talked about his aspirations for the future after he was appointed. He brought a very clear philosophy to the job:

'In the late sixties some of the students in my old school St Nathy's College, Ballaghaderreen gave a bit of a hiding to some younger pupils. As he sought to resolve the disciplinary issues the Dean of Studies Father James Gavigan remarked: "If you want to know what a person is like give them authority."

'I have learned that attitude is more than ability, that the motives you have are more important than brains; the courage you have is much more important than all the ingenuity you can gather and that the most important thing of all is that your heart is in the right place.

'The late Oscar Traynor when he was Minister for Defence was invited to speak at the commissioning service for the new army officers. Given the tradition of long speeches everyone was surprised that his speech consisted of just four sentences: "Congratulations on receiving your commission from the president. I understand you have a week off – enjoy it. You have now got weight – pull it. Don't throw it around." Those last two remarks enunciated a very helpful philosophy for someone taking on a challenging leadership role. It certainly resonates with my prejudices.'

He was thrilled to have reached the top of the Defence Forces:

'When I joined the cadet school back in 1965 I could never dreamed I would end up in this position. I would be lying if I said I was not very proud to have been promoted to this post. I know this might sound vain but it really does mean a lot.

'I honestly believe though it is not about me. We have a very negative attitude to power. I prefer to think more in terms of influence and I come to the job not just with a lot of hopes but with a number of specific targets and objectives. I know the economic recession will bring tough times for many people in the army and there will be very unpalatable decisions to be taken but I would like to think that in the coming years I can do some good for the betterment of the army and maybe, in a small way, Ireland as a whole.'

There was just one tiny tinge of regret as he climbed to the summit of army life in a precise, elongated arc: 'I would loved my father to have seen it. He would have been incredibly proud of me. I have been incredibly lucky in my career and each time something wonderful happens I find myself thinking: if my father could see me now.'

Did you ever kill a man?

One of the occupational hazards of such a long career in the army was Earley was often asked: 'Did you ever kill a man?' His tactic was to deflect attention by telling an apocryphal story about a Roscommon soldier:

'He was an officer in the British army during World War 11. At one stage he captured a German officer. They began to talk to each other. It emerged that the German had lived in Ireland for a few years while his father worked on the dam in Ard na Cruishe. When he heard that his captor was from Roscommon he said: "I visited all the counties in the west of Ireland but I really loved Roscommon. It is on the Shannon and a beautiful place."

'After much pleading the Roscommon man agreed to let his captive go free. He explained though, that if anybody saw him releasing the German he would be court-martialled and shot. He said he would turn his back and count to 10 and if the German were out of sight he wouldn't bother pursuing him. The count completed he turned around. The "enemy soldier" stood on a hill and waved down to him. The Roscommon man waved backed up. Then without any warning the German shouted: "Up Mayo." The Roscommon man shot him on the spot.

'As he stood there holding his smoking rifle in his hand he said aloud: "After he said that, sure I had to kill him". '

Poet's corner

After Dermot's death the family received hundreds of letters from people in all walks of life from all over the country. Many of them came from people who had served with him in the Defence Forces. Among them was an *Ode to Lt General Dermot Earley* by Private Peter McGuinness:

I served with General Earley
In the hills of South Lebanon
His gallant leadership he did show
To each and everyone
A soldier, a leader, and gentleman, a friend
A man we were proud to serve with
Right up to the very end
We salute you General Earley
A standard high you did set
Your presence on this earth
A time we will never forget.

Every year since Dermot's death one of his former colleagues places flowers on his grave on his birthday. A small incident which tells a big story of the respect he commanded.

Supertrooper

The army was a huge part of who Dermot was: 'I think of the army in the way I think of the GAA. We are part of a family. Even your career is over in both you still belong to them. I thought of that day when I heard the awful news of Ronan Stewart when he fell to his death in Boston when scaffolding he was working on collapsed. He had been a member of the Defence Forces but was on pre discharge leave but I was very saddened by the news because in my mind he was still one of us. His friend Shane McGettigan also lost his life in the accident. I was very aware of who Shane was, not only because he was the son of Charlie of Eurovision fame, but because he was playing for Leitrim and was a young man with a great future. The loss of two young lives was such a tragedy and they leave a huge gap in the lives of those who loved them.

'The reason I admire the people who make up the Defence Forces so much can be summed up in one word: dedication. These are women and men who put their lives on the line in the interest of others. As I talk I can see myself standing in Beirut airport and bodies being flown. I can also see in my mind the cold dark winter evenings in Dublin airport, meeting the corpses of heroic Irish soldiers who had shed their lives for the cause of peace.

'The Bible tells us that greater love hath no man than he who lays down his life for his friend. To me greater heroism has no woman or man who lay down their lives for their country. It fills me with pride to see so many of our soldiers who have been and continue to be willing to put their lives on the line.'

The day after Dermot's death in his office in the army barracks in Athlone Brigadier General Gerry Hegarty of the fourth Western Brigade paid tribute to a fallen colleague: 'Dermot was a few years ahead of me but when we joined he was an inspiration to us because he was such a big name nationally because of his profile in the GAA. He was someone we looked up to because of the kind of man he was. As my career in the army developed I saw how he grew into such a distinguished army officer.

'I remember in 2001 briefing a group of journalists and telling them that where the Irish peacekeepers were was where the sun never set – because we were all over the world. It is something to be proud of and Dermot more than played his part in that respect.'

9

Don't F**k It Up

'You are going to the Middle East.'

In April 1975 Dermot Earley had been totally unexpectedly summonsed from the army training ground in the Glen of Imaal and instructed to report back to the Curragh immediately. He expected the worst. Instead without any pleasantries he received this simple matter of fact statement.

On 2 July, he set off on a two-year stint on peacekeeping duties to take up his post as a military observer with the United Nations Troop Supervision Organisation on the Golan Heights. He was conscious of fitting into a wider story: 'Eighty five Irish soldiers in the last 50 years have made the ultimate sacrifice with their lives in the cause of Ireland's peacekeeping missions abroad and the way in which experience in locations such as Angola, Cambodia, Central America, Iran-Iraq, Kuwait, Afghanistan and most recently Chad has enabled Ireland to become world leaders in peace-keeping activities.

'Perhaps the most significant episode in the last 50 years was our mission to the Congo in 1960 which captivated the attention of the Irish public, attracting enormous media attention at the time; and this interest intensified with the tragic death of Irish soldiers in the course of their duty and the way in which they became martyrs for the cause of peace. Their return from duty touched a deep chord in the psyche of the Irish people. Few events in the last 50 years have precipitated such a groundswell of sympathy. Their funerals were said to be the biggest seen in Ireland since the burial of Michael Collins.'

Desert storms

In 1967 Israel invaded Syria. The invasion became popularly known as 'the Six days War'. The Israelis had gone into Syria and pushed towards the capital, Damascus. They also went into the Sinai desert and pushed on towards the Suez Canal. When that war ended, the Golan Heights was in the hands of Israel.

This position remained until a further war in 1973 when Egypt, Syrian and the Arabian countries attacked Israel. When that war ended a new situation existed which led to the creation of an area of separation between both Syrian and Israeli armies. The result was that a force of Israelis and Syrians faced each other with the UN in between.

A feature of the area was that the landscape was despoiled by war debris. An intrinsic part of Earley's observation requirement was the patrolling of the separated area, which was a dangerous activity because of the prevalence of landmines: 'On one occasion I saw a mine going off under a herd of goats and two or three of them were killed. Once I saw a donkey being blown up. There were a number of occasions when I was involved in arranging emergency hospital relief for shepherds, in some cases, young boys or girls who were very badly injured by mines exploding. My task was to use our communications system to arrange emergency medical evacuations.

'To a casual observer there was a relaxed atmosphere and little danger of hostilities breaking out. But beneath the calm exterior a deep distrust remained which led to sporadic bouts of tension. In such a volatile atmosphere, the smallest incident could spark a major crisis, even all out war. For example, some shepherds might move too close to the fence on the Israeli side. The Israelis would interpret this as an attempt to test their defences and warning shots would be fired to keep the shepherds away. On one occasion shots resulted in the death of a shepherd in a situation close to me.

'One time there was a flurry of activity on the Israeli side and we had no idea what was going on. It was only when we listened to a report on the BBC World Service that day that we discovered what had happened. The Israeli army had intercepted an infiltration of what the Israelis called "terrorists" and that group was killed.

'Another day I remember carrying out a fortnightly inspection of the military forces when I saw somebody scrambling for cover. The radar screens picked up incoming aircraft and sure enough, almost immediately a Mig fighter came very close to the Israeli side of the ceasefire line and then turned away. This was an attempt to test the Israelis and to see what the Israeli response might be. After that there was an all out alert by the Israeli soldiers. Had these aircraft crossed even one centimeter of their borderline, all hell would have broken loose.

'One of the first things that grabbed my attention was the sight of two armies being deployed against one another. You can imagine what it must be like, but you really have to experience it for yourself. The tragedy that war brings was something I learned at first hand, particularly the cruel division of families which meant that they could only communicate with each other through a megaphone.'

Penalty points

Earley's sporting interest was to help him professionally: 'Some of my colleagues and I went on an inspection on the Syrian side of the Golan Heights and we went to a particular camp where the Commander would not allow us to inspect. There was consternation when we were discovered and we were marched to the Commander's tent.

'There he had pictures of many beautiful girls on the wall and he also had pictures of great soccer players particularly goalkeepers from England and Europe. Immediately the conversation turned to football. The next thing a football was produced from behind a desk. The Commander explained that he was a goalkeeper himself and he invited them outside to show off his skills. Goals were set up and a penalty competition was introduced. As the Commander stood tall and erect in the goal his "goal-posts" were two stones, just like we used in the west of Ireland years ago.

'The event had caught the imagination of the camp and everybody was crowding around the "pitch". There was a great carnival atmosphere. An Irish officer was designated as the penalty taker. One of the other observers whispered into his ear saying, "Perhaps on this an occasion you should miss." The penalty taker faced a tricky situation. If he scored the Commander would be embarrassed. He did not look very agile. His ability might not match his interest. The easiest kick for a goalie to save is a shot that is waist high and is right in the centre of the goal. The ball can be hit very hard but all the keeper has to do is to stand up straight and put up his hands. With this in mind the Irish officer blasted the ball straight at the Commander. It looked like a great save and he was delighted. All the Syrian soldiers were ecstatic; it was like winning the World Cup itself.

'That penalty save completely diffused a potentially difficult decision. The Commander was higher in the estimation of his troops than ever before and savoured his moment of glory. The UN officers left confident in the knowledge that relations would be smoother with that particular camp in the foreseeable future.'

Earley quickly learned the diplomatic skills that were needed on a mission like this:

'On one of my first missions I was accompanied by a Liaison Officer who was due to take charge of our encounter with the Israeli Commander we were due to meet. The conversation went well until we were leaving and the Israeli officer made a simple request. He politely asked if one of his officers might be given a lift in the UN vehicle to the first town on our way back. Taking the passenger would not have involved us in any detour. Our man made a big scene about it and wouldn't let him travel with us. I felt that it was a grave mistake. Here we were trying to win their support but metaphorically we were slapping them in the face. The right course would have been to say certainly. Should other approaches be made requesting greater favours, then you would have to reconsider and exercise your judgement. The observer in question outlined in no uncertain terms the reason for his refusal. Although he was following the letter of the law I felt the correct option in peacekeeping terms would have been to accede to his request.

'There was another day when we had to cross into Syria from Israel. This necessitated going through four checkpoint gates, initially an Israeli gate, then a UN gate, then a second UN gate, and finally a Syrian gate. Sometimes there could be a delay at a particular gate and the officer I was travelling with got extremely impatient, even aggressive, with the Israelis. That impatience should never have been expressed. In practical terms all that was all that was achieved was another delay. However, if you saw there was a problem and you said you appreciated their problem, then ninety-nine times out of a hundred you were let through quickly. It's all about patience and approach.'

The City of David

Mary was at her husband's side on that tour. It was a momentous period for them as they became first time parents. The birth took place in the Arab quarter of Jerusalem. Arabic protocol dictated that the father should not present at the birth.

Earley paced anxiously up and down in the front garden he heard his name being shouted from the window. When the news emerged that David was born he raced up the stairs to see his new son being wheeled out of the delivery room on a trolley. A score of attendants shouted: 'Not allowed. Not allowed,' But the new Dad turned a deaf ear. Later Earley would be struck by the cultural differences in his temporary home. An Arabic woman who had her fourth daughter left the hospital in floods of tears because she had not given birth to a son.

Euphoria was too mild a term to describe the elation and exhilaration he felt, scarcely able to contain his joy. No words can adequately convey his feelings. It was not just parental pride. It was a sense of belonging to a new family unit of being part of something special.

There are moments when it seems the gods are on your side - when nothing can possibly go wrong. A lifetime seemed to be crowded into the space of a second.

Thoughts of being the perfect parents were uppermost in their minds when they made the journey home from hospital. It was a voyage into the unknown. The life of the first time parent is a curious and fascinating mixture of happiness and stress. The pleasure of the little, coy smiles, the sheer bliss of holding the baby in their arms, the excitement of showing off the baby to relatives and friends is balanced off by worrying about ensuring that the baby is neither too hot or too cold, sleepless nights with crying and feedings, dirty nappies and, most alarmingly, the fear of the frail new creature getting ill.

Brothers in arms

Much of Earley's work on that tour was collaborative. He developed a lasting relationship with an officer from Austria. The story of their friendship embodies the close relationship, which develops between peacekeepers:

'We were both based in Tiberius at the time and we worked closely together. His wife was an exceptionally beautiful blonde lady who became friends with Mary. One night he and I were in total darkness in our observation point. We had to disconnect all our equipment because there was a horrendous thunderstorm and we were afraid that if lightning struck our masts we could lose our radio. There was no communication with base until the raging storm had subsided.

'We discussed our families, our hobbies and our upbringing, the Austria that he grew up in and the West of Ireland; finally the discussion moved on to meeting our wives. He asked me if I ever met my wife's father. I explained that unfortunately he had died sometime before I met her, God rest him.

'I repeated his question and he said no. Then he paused and I detected hesitancy as he deliberated whether he should elaborate further or not. I didn't prompt or say anything. After a while he said: "My wife's father was a Russian soldier who came to Berlin during World War 11 and raped my wife's mother. As a result of that rape my wife was born." The fact that he had shared such an intimate secret testifies to the close bond that develops between people in such a tense situation.'

A bedside companion

Despite the demands of his challenging job and the adjustment of being a first time Dad Dermot had one other mission:

'In my luggage from Ireland pride of place was a Gaelic football. We had thick walls around the living accommodation. Every day I took out the ball and kicked the ball against the walls from different directions to see if I could stop it from passing me by. If there was a flat area there was conducive to running and would allow me to run a solo run for a mile or two up the road, I would do so. One thing I had to be very aware of was not to cause panic to either the Israeli or Syrian forces. There was a very real danger that the conflicting sides might misinterpret a running figure for an enemy and take a shot.

'To my horror one day the ball took a bad bounce and went down the valley and I could see it a few hundred feet below. Should I risk climbing down a hazardous path or should I forget the ball? I had the vision of the Roscommon jersey in my mind and that decided it for me. I retrieved the ball in a climb that was physically shattering rather than dangerous with the sweat pouring out of me and I decided to do this climb every day would be a great way to get fit. Whenever I was feeling lazy I deliberately forced myself into the climb by kicking the ball down the valley. It kept me in shape.'

Earley's peacekeeping mission at the time was enthusiastically supported by four of the Connacht counties as Galway's star midfielder Brian Talty acknowledges:

'We played Roscommon in a Connacht final in 1976 while

Dermot was abroad and it was like Hamlet without the prince. Every year we would keep an eye on the papers hoping to read that Dermot was going abroad on peacekeeping duty that year. When he came back in 1977 the Rossies beat us narrowly in the Connacht final, with Dermot starring as was his wont, and we all wished he could have stayed in the Middle East for a few more months!'

Tragedy

Talty's wish would be granted in 1982 when Earley made his second peacekeeping mission in the Lebanon. His role was to be Staff Officer with responsibility for administration, morale and discipline. He hoped for a gentle start to find his feet but it was not to be.

Within hours three Irish soldiers were killed as they manned an observation post. One of the widows of the soldiers was expecting a baby that her husband would never see:

'It was a terrible shock to us all as well as a horrific tragedy for three grieving families. My main priority was to take practical steps to sustain and improve morale, for example, to ensure that soldiers got mail quickly. If a soldier felt badly and came to me requesting a personal call home, I would arrange that immediately, or at least at the first available opportunity. There could have been many reasons for this, such as family bereavement. The priority was to keep both soldiers and family happy.

'For individual soldiers events like birthdays, First Holy Communions, and anniversaries can be particularly tough. A trying time for everybody is when mail goes astray. A week goes by and regular letter or letters from home fail to arrive. People on the ground and those at home can get very lonely.

'The worst time of all is Christmas. People become very conscious of missing their families at that time. The army makes every possible effort to recreate the type of Christmas atmosphere you would experience at home but this is very difficult in a hot climate. Depression was a constant threat especially when people got bad news like a relationship break-up. You had to be very attentive for signs of death by suicide in extreme cases.

'You have to remember that there was no mobile phones then, let alone emails or social media. The one positive development that improved our quality of life at the time was the advent of video. We could see programmes, football matches and current affairs shortly after they had been transmitted. This helped to boost morale.'

On that trip Earley would face tense situations: 'One day in the village of Bara-Shiit in South Lebanon I was in a very tense situation. Our position had been attacked. Grenades had been thrown at it. The base was now secure but a threat existed of the firing of a rocket-propelled grenade at the location.

'As I was looking through the binoculars, two Israeli aircraft flew high overhead. I did not see or hear them fly over because they were flying faster than the speed of sound. Of course that created a sonic boom. When I heard it I was sure that our position had been hit. There was definitely a cold-sweat down my back and I can feel it now down my backbone. Then I realised what had happened. Relief was great but it was impossible to describe the tension, the fear, and the concern for my colleagues.

'Many people will know Paul Brady's marvellous song *The Island* in which he talks about the conflict in Lebanon. He sings about the women and children dying in the street. At its worst this was a horrific conflict.'

Apart from missing out on playing for Roscommon, Earley would pay a high personal cost for his trip: 'When I came home it was great to see Mary and the children again. The three boys were looking at me with great expectancy, wanting to hear about Lebanon. Paula was skipping with excitement. Little Anne-Marie, who was only two at the time, didn't want to know me at all and every time I turned my attention towards her she just ignored me and turned away. There was fear in her eyes and she had no idea who this stranger was. It is a pretty humbling and wounding experience to be treated like a stranger by your own daughter. These are the problems anybody who is away for a long time has to cope with. To make the adjustment back to your family is difficult.'

Start spreading the news

Four years later he broke the news to the family that he was on the move again but this time he got a much more enthusiastic reaction: 'I was appointed Assistant Military Advisor to the Secretary-General to the Secretary-General of the UN, Mr. Javier Perez de Cuellar for what ended up as a four year appointment. When I went home that evening, I managed to keep the news to myself until after dinner and then I said: "I have news". There was intense curiosity. I said: "I am going overseas in June." Nobody spoke. Then I said: "And you were all coming with me." There was great excitement. I said: "We are going to New York." David shouted out immediately: "The Giants". I will never forget it. He had been watching American football and I could see his brain working overtime that he would get the chance to see them in the flesh.'

Flying over New York City was an incredibly thrilling experience for the six Earley children as they were awestruck at its enormity. Their father would recall that sensation when he heard former Mayo star Anthony 'fat Larry' Finnerty's reaction flying in over New York: 'Jaysus lads, these boys have some pick to choose from.'

The family quickly settled in to their new environment. The great thing about the time in America for Conor Earley was that he got much less homework than he would have at home. There was though a scary experience awaiting his father:

'Within three days I began experiencing dizzy spells. These spells became more frequent and more intense with each passing day. Coming out of the elevator I would feel unbalanced. To the outside world I was walking like a drunkard. While working in my office I would suddenly have to cling to the desk, to stop myself from keeling over. I was genuinely worried I would have to be sent home to Ireland on health grounds after seven days of this. Then my predecessor in the role John Ryan casually mentioned at the end of one of our many briefing meetings: "Oh, by the way, one of the things that happened to me when I came here first was that I got unbalanced from travelling so often in the elevators. I thought I would have to be sent home."

'Two days later I had the last of my dizzy spells. My office was on the 36th floor of the giant building so the elevator was an integral part of my working day. The Secretary-General was two floors above me.'

A tale of two cities

What is the most effective summary of Earley's time in the UN? It was the best of times. It was the worst of times.

In many ways it was a great period professionally particularly because he got on well with Perez de Cuellar:

'He worked very long days and was constantly in meetings and was continuously in demand. There was a sort of matter-of-factness about all meetings with him. You would meet him on the corridor and you would be asked for an input from your work. No pleasantries were exchanged. Everything moved so fast, which allowed him no opportunities for small talk. Every second counted.

'In all meetings he conducted himself in a very formal manner. He went around the table and shook hands with everybody, regardless of whether he had met them three times already that day or never met them before. As he got to know me he departed from normal procedure at meetings. For some reason he would always take me by my elbow, give it a squeeze and say: "My man."'

Although Earley was ultimately answerable to de Cuellar, the man he normally reported to was Marrack Goulding, Under Secretary-General for Special Political Affairs with responsibility for peacekeeping:

'We worked closely together for four years. A lot of the time I travelled on peacekeeping missions I went with him. He was British so he used cricket metaphors a lot.

'Once when we were negotiating in the Iranians after a lengthy session in which he seemed to be going nowhere, almost unbelievably the Iranian deputy Foreign Minister left an opening. I remember that when the opening came, it was like going for a goal. I was ready to pounce in and so was Goulding. Marrack took the opening and gained a great point. In our discussion afterwards he said: "I hit him for six."

'Later that night we were negotiating with a different group on a similar issue. There was an interval for tea and Goulding casually asked the head of the Iranian delegation if he had ever been to England. "Oh yes, I was there in 1972," came the instant reply. "How long did you stay?" "Oh I was deported after two hours." Goulding went purple with embarrassment. He looked over at me and whispered: "I have just been clean bowled."'

A regular part of Earley's duties was to brief visiting dignitaries:

'Probably the most famous was with a man who was to go on to achieve worldwide recognition during the Gulf War, Colin Powell. Two weeks later he became Chairman of the Joint Chiefs of Staff.

'I was very taken with him. He was the first African-American in that role. I was impressed by his confidence. He was a fine, tall and fit-looking man. For the Supreme Commander of the US forces, he did not expect special treatment. His questions were precise and to the point, and tidied up areas that I had not really clarified. He was easy to understand. I remember especially the firmness of his handshake. I can't remember how it came up but I found out he's an Abba fan!

'Two weeks later I briefed another senior US officer came for a briefing and I opened the discussion by saying he had come four weeks too late. I told him Colin Powell had been with me and now he was Chief of Staff.'

The high points of his four years in the UN were his involvement in the independence of Namibia from South Africa, a ceasefire in Angola, dealings with the Iraqi government and be around for the awarding of a Nobel Peace Prize to the UN in 1988, standing in for the Secretary-General at one of the ceremonies. One incident stood out for him: 'I was involved in negotiating an end to the Angolan civil war. In the immediate aftermath, during the course of a dinner in Lisbon with Angolan leaders and international statesmen, I made what was termed "a stirring speech" about what the future held for Angola. A Portuguese academic with a keen interest in the peace process passed me a note, which read: "You have it. Don't f**k it up".'

In every life some rain must fall. Earley had plenty of it in those four years:

'The lowest points were when I would arrive in the morning and see a cable informing me that a UN peace-keeping soldier had been shot or blown up. Immediately you would think of a grieving family at home. Then you would have to brief the Ambassador of that country. Sometimes, the notification of casualty might indicate on the bottom that the next of kin were not informed. I had to ensure that he press did not get that information until the next of kin were informed.'

Another big frustration was the unwillingness of some countries to co-operate fully with the UN: 'The Iranians were very difficult to deal with. I think they distrusted the UN. It took a long time for them out see that we were there for their good. It was not helped by some incidents that took place with our observers. Alcohol is banned in Iran. A non-Irish observer acquired alcohol and in a drunken state pulled down a lot of placards of the Ayatollah. He was arrested but because of his semi-diplomatic status he was released. This caused a lot of resentment.

'The other thing you saw was fear. That was particularly evident from the children. You might see them running with a tyre and steering it with a stick. Your attention would be drawn to their laughter. Any of us who had children ourselves might make a friendly, playful gesture in their direction. But they would flee immediately and there would be terror in their faces.

'In war when you move, you have to move quickly. You are running all the time. People become programmed to run. When the war ends and the UN moves in, people continue to run. Women and children catch hands and run at the sight of strangers. It is hard for people to learn to trust again.'

The Mother of All Battles

The big event in Earley's time in the UN was the Gulf War: 'Even Saddam Hussein must have foreseen the potential catastrophic consequences, massive loss of life, and the huge destruction of a war. I was convinced that he would step back from the brink. When the war began I was shocked to the very core.

'My main contact was to our existing personnel in the Middle East, namely the Golan Heights, in Israel, and with our mission in Cyprus. We were peripheral while the war was going on. Our main task was to prepare plans for some kind of buffer zone between Iraq and Kuwait. I was watching the television for news. CNN were bringing us "up to the second" actual live footage of the conflict. The scary thing was that some of the briefings that were given by the US forces were drawn from CNN reports. It was the first time the world had witnessed a war as a soap opera.'

After the war ended, Earley had to go back to the Gulf to supervise the introduction of peacekeeping forces and to deal with the problem of the Kurdish refugees. The memory of his flight over the battlefield would forever remain entrenched on his brain:

'It was an awesome sight to look down on the battlefield. It was frightening and alarming to see that all of this could happen and to see that it did happen; it was very sad, almost unreal.

'The first thing that struck me was the pollution from the massive oil wells. There were seven hundred burning oil wells and they clouded the skies with their fumes, spewing massive thick clouds of pollution into the air. At the time I was there, the wind was taking it in one huge cloud, covering hundreds of miles and carrying it eastward. Just before that it had gone southwards and had engulfed the city of Kuwait and had turned midday almost into midnight.

'Bodies still lay on the ground. Helmets had obviously fallen from the head as the face was buried in the sand. A boot stood standing on its own. You wondered who owned it and where was that person now.

'Further up the desert and you came to a crossroads just north of Kuwait City, just leading into Iraq where at some stage in the last few days of the war there was a massive withdrawal of the Iraqi forces. They had been caught by a coalition forces air strike. I have never seen such destruction. The vehicles seemed to be piled up on the junction. They lay in a monstrous mess of twisted metal, shattered tanks and burned out cabs. In all the chaos perhaps there was a tank in the middle, which had not been touched at all, that had escaped the destruction. When you saw all this you wondered what the loss of life in this area must have been.

'Then as you moved further north you saw the sand blowing below. You saw minefields appearing as the sand blew away. In the distance you could see shepherds coming out with their flocks and carry on as they had for hundreds of years before the battle took place. You wondered how they were going to survive with all the war debris and all the unexploded mines.

'I had been to Kuwait before the war had broken out. I had flown from Tehran to Kuwait, having been involved in the negotiations to end the Iran-Iraq war. Here was a magnificent city. Then to return after the war and see the scars. The walls were covered with a horrible blackness. The hotel where I had stayed during my first visit was now totally burned out. It was just a shell. All the windows were gone. The area that I had walked around the first time was now almost impassable with all the rubble. It was impossible to comprehend.'

A Living Hell

The Kurdish problem predated the war. The Iraqi defence minister, Ali Hassan al Majid, spearheaded a campaign of genocide against the Kurds. He was known to the Kurdish people as 'Ali of the Chemicals'. In 1988 he ordered the dropping of chemical bombs on the town of Halabja. More than 5,500 people lost their lives in that one incident. In addition people were tortured in groups so that when one broke down and confessed, others would follow suit:

'I had flown over northern Iraq to look at the ceasefire line between Iran and Iraq and saw the villages that had been destroyed by the Iraqi forces and the purge against the Kurds. The villages were absolutely flattened. The houses were lying like scattered stones on the ground. Then you saw how isolated the Kurds were. They were so vulnerable.

'I had seen pictures of Saddam Hussein's assaults on the Kurds. One picture stands out in my mind. It appeared in *Time* magazine shortly after that particular assault on the Kurds. A father and his child lay dead on the ground having being gassed. It appeared as if he was carrying the baby and as he breathed in the air he died and the baby fell from his hands and rolled on the ground. The baby lay beside his head. Both of them looked in perfect condition but both were victims of chemical weapons.'

For the refugees Earley was trying to help, life had become a living hell: 'Remember all their difficulties. They lost their homes. They often had nowhere to lay their weary heads at night. The belongings that you have are in all a bag over your shoulder, a plastic bag with a few bits and pieces tied with a string. As they went along they probably lost some of these possessions. They were not sure if they would have food that night or next morning. The babies or very young children might not be able to walk and would have to be carried along distances in difficult situations. Some of those who could walk might not have shoes. Some might have slippers walking through the mud. Others might have sandals, like Irish children might wear on hot summer days, during the torrential rains that were falling in the wintertime.

'In the southern part of Iraq you would see the sand blowing in small tornadoes swirling around. Women tried to protect their children by putting cloaks around their faces to prevent the sand from blowing against them. They had no homes to go. Perhaps half of the family was missing. The absence of a father or mother's care would be clearly visible in the eyes of the children as they looked with bulging eyes in wonder. They were wondering what all the strangers were doing around them.

'The other thing I remember was the lines on people's faces. They had been through so much and that was reflected in their faces. The laughter was gone from their eyes. I had seen this one before in Iran, in a small village right on the battlefield, when I went there at the end of the Iran-Iraq war. There was an emptiness in the back of peoples' eyes. They had a total loss of belief in society and in all institutions.'

From a distance

It is often said that the first casualty of war is the truth but whose truths? Such is the complexity of the conflict that it is difficult, if not impossible, to identify the 'good guys and bad guys'. In the thousands of articles which have attempted to analyse the source of the conflict and the search for a political or military solution the human cost of the war sometimes does not get the attention it deserves. Such is the enormity of the horror that it is virtually impossible for any eyewitness to speak dispassionately about the topic.

Dermot talked about football with an addict's passion. Asking him about his memories of the atrocities he witnessed in conflict zones during those four years was likely suddenly being introduced to a stranger. His reticence spoke volumes when contrasted with his easy affability conversing about football. All he offered was hints of the horrors he witnessed. In those moments there was vulnerability about him, a sadness that clinged to him and a sense that his mind often travelled in a land uninhabited by the rest of us. It was not difficult to imagine voices, which run through his head like silver bullets, screaming memories into the caverns of his mind, the primitive regions of the unconscious and beyond. When pressed about the worst atrocity he had witnessed, he shook his had and said softly, "I don't walk to talk about it." He did have some general observations:

'I think the first thing I noticed when we got into a conflict zone was that nobody smiled at all. There was this sort of pain on people's faces as if they had a burden they carried with them.

'In a refugee camp in this troubled country there is often no living just existence. Around the country death stalks the roads and ditches. There are bodies all over the place, laid out side-by-side by the road - bodies and limbs blown away, bloodied and awful. Whether or not the country was previously divisible between political groupings, the effect of the genocide is to confirm a genuine gulf - between those who were the targets of murder and those who did the murdering. It is in the interests of the leaders on both "sides" to spread their murderous hate. Babies are often the only survivors with the energy to cry.'

Waging war

The four years in the United Nations deepened Earley's commitment to the cause of peace. However, it also prompted him to believe that we needed a new war – the war on poverty: 'The thing I saw most of all was poverty. You could go into any of the magnificent palaces, such as that of the King of Morocco but when you came out and saw the Bedouins roaming with their camels.'

In some countries incredible wealth and total poverty went side-by-side: 'In South Africa I visited Capetown where I saw the southern tip of the Cape of Good Hope. The line where the Indian and the Atlantic Oceans meet was pointed out to you. What was not pointed out were the shantytowns, tin shacks where people clung on to life by a thread. Immediately, my mind flashed back to visiting the local supermarket the day before, to buy some toothpaste. Outside, there were black girls, half-naked, begging. We really have no idea in Ireland about absolute poverty.

'From the moment I entered the baggage area of the airport in these countries I was confronted by intense poverty. To see this on television is akin to watching *The Simpsons*. You say to yourself this can not really happen. But when the stark reality is but feet away from you, it is frightening in the extreme.'

Many of his accounts of poverty in conflict zones in a variety of countries have a depressing similarity. It seems that the lot of the poor is to live frugally on the crumbs from the wealthy elite's tables.

In these places all seem soaked in a heavy despondency as if some totally melancholy spirit brooded over the place. Flies feast on the sea of slurry, and the buzz of their relish produces a faint hum in the air. Poverty is sucking the vitality out of it as a bee sucks honey out of a flower. The slum, foul smelling and decrepit, is a monument to broken hearts and foiled aspirations, to innumerable tales of sadness and dawning shreds of hope. It is easy to imagine that the stinking stench would upset the stomach of a horse.

There are thousands like it throughout conflict zones, and every one tells the same story. Illness. Hunger. The death of hope. A person, it is held, can become accustomed to anything, but poverty for these people is a recurring nightmare. Here, as in most places, money or more precisely the lack of it, makes all the difference. It is difficult not to succumb to a great sense of the desolation of life which sweeps all round like a tidal wave, drowning all in its blackness.

Eyewitness testimony

After he returned from his four years in New York, Dermot continued to keep an eye on the burning issue of the day. A blot on the face of humanity. That is the only description, which adequately describes the bloodbath, which took place in former Yugoslavia where society was drawn into a web of ever-increasing intolerance, bigotry and racial tensions. The international community largely responded in the early stages by not responding.

Dermot had an insatiable thirst to find out all he could about any conflict. A mutual friend arranged for him to get a private meeting in a personal capacity with an eyewitness to the events. This was his personal perspective on the conflict:

The Serbian tanks first appeared on the streets in May 1991. At that stage we didn't know we were at war. It was only when the tanks surrounded our Croatian town, with a population of just 44,000 that we knew we were in a war situation. We had no army and virtually no communication with the outside world. Within a few months we had run out of food. We had only grass to eat. If you were lucky you had fried dog food and grass. If you are starving to death it tastes very good. On November 15 of that year we surrendered. We were starved. We were marched out at gunpoint and then the slaughter begun. The Jewish population no longer exists there. It was total extermination.

After we surrendered the torture began immediately. There was a massacre all the way as the troops advanced. The people were separated into three groups, men, women and children. The men were all killed. The women were raped. It was impossible to keep up with all the killing. I've heard people since talking about ethnic cleansing. This is not a Serb term but a media phrase. It is a nice way of saying genocide but ethnic cleansing is extermination.

We were put in what were called internment camps. In reality they were concentration and slave labour camps. In my case they took my fingernails out and burned me with cigarettes. Their tactic was to kill people in the most cruel way possible - piece-by-piece. They sliced people up, cut off their noses, then stopped, cut off the lips, then stopped, cut off the fingers, stopped again, then the eyes were cut out and they stopped again. They used stop-start tactics in their torture because there was more pain that way. When they got tired they killed people.

The television cameras showed a mass grave of 5000 people.

That's extermination. In one building they put 900 people and took their knives into it and did their business. Another time they put 300 people in a field and did the same. I saw two ten-year-old girls running into a building in search of safety. The soldiers hurled a flame-thrower into the building and burned them alive. I saw one little boy being raped and they put bayonets through his eyes.

They forced us to dig our own graves and while we were digging they continued to torture people just for the fun of it, but by the end they were very drunk. When we were put into the grave they started shooting but sometimes the bullets went over the intended victim's heads. I was one of the few lucky ones who fell into that category and when darkness fell I was able to crawl out and make my escape. It's a blur now.

You had no feelings. It sounds terrible but emotionally you were numb. It was over. We fought and lost. Death was inevitable. It was over. You knew you had to die and you just prayed to God that your torture would be short and that you died quickly.

We knew that they would want to take revenge on the men and that we would all be killed but in our worst nightmares we never thought the women and the children would be butchered.

We got so many promises but no help. All that came was the Prince of Death. The Jews in particular were very concerned before we surrendered and wanted to try and escape. They thought the Serbs were like the Nazis. To my shame I persuaded the sixty of them to stay because I told them that the UN would surely come. I reminded them of how quickly the UN had intervened in Kuwait. They believed me but no one came and they all died. I can assure you that if you persuaded sixty people, including 30 children and 10 women to stay and all were killed you would feel very guilty.

When the international community eventually did get involved in former Yugoslavia Dermot was proud that Commandant Colm Doyle, an Irish officer, was the special representative of Lord Carrington in Sarajevo for the EC:

'Colm was in my senior class in the cadet school. I know him well. He has a great understanding of what conflict is about. He is a very personable man, ideally suited to conduct negotiations to achieve a cease-fire. He made great efforts to negotiate a cessation of hostilities and also to see if the ingredients were in place for a peacekeeping mission.

'One of the things that Colm's position in Sarajevo reflects is the quality of our education system in the army. Our senior Irish officers have the ability to go into any peace-keeping job and do it well.'

Emotional intelligence

Earley was appointed as battalion commander for a six-month tour of Lebanon in 1997. He was in charge of the full Irish contingent.

One term I never heard Dermot use was emotional intelligence. I spent a week with him on that tour while making a documentary for Shannonside radio. It was then I really saw that the secret of Dermot's success in the army and in life was in large measure to his own exceptional emotional intelligence.

This was most clearly evident when he left his own camp and visited soldiers in the outlying camps. Every soldier, regardless of rank, got individual attention with the firm handshake and the big smile and all were addressed by their first name. The big GAA supports were given some banter, those with sick relatives at home got a quiet sympathetic word, and those new first time parents were given words of solace and encouragement.

At one stage out of the corner of his eye he spotted a young soldier who was cleaning the toilets. Immediately he made a beeline for him. I had seen Dermot engage with two previous Taoisigh but neither was greeted with more genuine warmth and interest than this young soldier.

Everyone he spoke with was made to feel important and valued and everybody went away feeling a bit better about themselves. That was the mark of the man.

He had an authority about him. He was a tall man but it was not his physical presence that did it. Nor was it that he spoke voluminously or loudly. If anything he was understated. What drew people to him is something intangible. By instinct he had an exceptionally firm grasp of human psychology and how to appeal to it and from that emanated presence, substance and the quality of strength without arrogance.

On that trip I kept a diary to try to capture a flavour of the tour. This is one of the entries:

3 September 1997

It was not quite mid-morning, but the sun is already high in the sky and humidity quite enervating. Harsh sunlight falls dully on rusty rooftops. A man drives his Mercedes car to an old farm shed. His wife gets out and opens the door. She re-emerges a few minutes later with a donkey and cart. The man sits in the shade and the woman goes to work in the field. She stops just once to serve her husband his lunch before taking a quick meal herself. Talk of equality of opportunity and women's liberation cuts little ice here. From his vantage position an Irish soldier of his observation post on the hill marvels at the juxtaposition of the progressive and the ancient and shakes his head before ruefully saying: 'There's 2000 years of evolutionary history missing there somewhere.'

Lebanon has a long history. It was mentioned as early as 3000 B.C. as a string of coastal cities with a heavily forested and thickly populated hinterland. Its inhabitants were a Semitic people, the Canaanites, whom the Greeks called Phoenicians in light of the purple (phoenix) dye they sold. The Greek poet, Homer, describes how Phoenician vessels carried Lebanese fruits and perfumes to Greece. Throughout the centuries such disparate groups as the Christian Crusaders, the Turks and the French have regularly invaded the country. In 1982 Israel invaded Lebanon with the grandiose name of 'Operation peace for Galilee' with the expressed purpose of destroying all 'terrorist' bases in South Lebanon. They laid siege to Beirut for eight weeks, after which Arafat evacuated his Palestinian militia from Lebanon.

Since 1978 Irish soldiers have played a central role in the United Nations Interim Force in Lebanon (UNIFIL). Irishbatt as the Irish Battalion is called, occupy territory in the South some of which is controlled by Israel.

Irishbatt are involved in the challenging and often hazardous task of maintaining peace and preserving stability. Two rival camps ensure the tension is ever present.

AMAL is a socio-political-religious movement founded by Imam Mousa Al Sadar in the early 1970s. It represents the majority of the Shiite population of Lebanon. AMAL means 'hope'. The AMAL are the most dominant political force in the Irishbatt area. Their military wing is engaged in resistance activity against the Israelis and their militia. The vast majority of the AMAL weaponry is of Soviet design. AMAL are considered as a more moderate grouping and are generally supportive of UNIFIL.

Hezbollah is a fundamentalist Shiite movement that is funded by Iran and facilitated by Syria. It means 'The Party of God.' It was founded in 1978 but did not come to prominence in Lebanon until the Israeli Invasion of 1982. Its main powerbase is in the Bekka Valley where most training and strategic planning is conducted. Much of the training is supervised by Iranian Revolutionary Guards from Iran. They are a fanatical minority but very active grouping with small cells in most villages. Their military wing Islamic Resistance is responsible for most of the resistance operations in the Irishbatt Area of Operations. They are not supportive of UNIFIL and resent the restriction imposed by UNIFIL on their activities.

It is a tragedy that the scars of war should hideously mar one of the most beautiful and spectacular landscapes in the world.

One example suffices to illustrate, i.e. Operation Grapes of Wrath. The operation, which consisted of a lengthy aerial, naval and land bombardment, was launched by Israel to try to limit ongoing Hezbollah attacks and to put pressure on the Lebanese and Syrian Governments to curb Hezbollah. A week later came the Qana massacre. Israeli artillery shells hit the Fijian headquarters of UNIFIL at Qana, killing approximately 110 Lebanese civilians sheltering in the area and four Fijian soldiers were injured in the attack.

The 81st Battalion is nicknamed GAABatt given the connections with the GAA given the prominence of the GAA connections on this trip. The Battalion Commander is former Roscommon footballing star Dermot Earley. Two of his deputies are Chris Moore who trained Meath to win minor and under-21 All-Irelands and another former Roscommon star Seán Kilbride.

The Irish have made the neighbourhood a home from home. The local shops are called 'The ILAC Centre' and 'Dunnes Stores' respectively. One is run by a Lebanese woman who speaks with a definite West of Ireland accent and who speaks more Irish than most of the soldiers. Cultural imperialism rules okay.

Radio is the Word. In the beginning was the word. Radio is essentially blind. Its images are a private treaty between commentator and listener. The audience must fill out the game with description and information. The commentator dabs words onto an aural canvas.

BBC World Service are featuring Manchester United's home tie with West Ham. The Irish soldiers who have a recreational break and the 81st Infantry Battalion are riveted. A poster on the wall states, 'Improve Morale. Increase Flogging.'

The previous Wednesday most of the United players had been on international duty and for the first 20 minutes they looked sluggish. Both Roy Keane and Denis Irwin had starred in Ireland's 2-1 victory over Lithuania in Vilnius, which effectively secured the Emerald Isle a play-off for a place in the 1998 World Cup.

Denis Irwin is left out for United's clash with high riding West Ham - in third place in the table. All of the pre-match talk is of their rising star Rio Ferdinand. It is Roy Keane though who steals the show. After 14 minutes he whacked a rasping shot against the post. Almost immediately though John Hartson puts the happy Hammers in front after a mix-up with Gary Pallister and Peter Schmeichel. Keane again has a go from distance and the ball takes a wicked deflection off a West Ham defender and flew into the net.

In the second half John Hartson squares up to Roy Keane, but the Corkman doesn't react. As if to signal his new maturity Keane even remonstrates with referee David Elleray when the striker is booked. 14 minutes from the end United got their winner when Paul Scholes heads a Gary Neville floated cross firmly inside the left hand post. Panic ensues when Peter Schmeichel inexplicably drops a 40 yarder from Unsworth, only to scramble on it on the goal line. The Irish soldiers hanging onto every word breathe a sigh of relief.

Moments later the siren goes off in the camp. Shelling has started nearby. A calm voice booms out over the address: 'Groundhog. Groundhog.' This is the cue for flight to the bunkers. The shelling is increasing. After a few minutes everyone is safely accounted for. As a calm descends among the Irish soldiers a discussion on United's form gives way to a preview of tomorrow's historic All-Ireland hurling final between Tipperary and Clare.

Two hours later it is safe to return. The night is dark now. Black clouds hang in bunches in the sky and from time to time bright streaks of lightning run across the heavens.

Word comes from the communications centre that the Hezbollah have assassinated two Israeli soldiers - raising the number of murdered Israeli soldiers this year to 33.

There is not a sound anywhere. Not a leaf stirs. Everywhere, there is a calm, a stillness, which spoke of peace but a tense night, is in prospect.

Crisis

Seán Kilbride had one very specific memory of that tour: 'There were times when things were very tense. We had a situation where we could not move on a road because there were many landmines, which stopped us from doing our job. Dermot negotiated a deal by which the mines would be cleared and we would be free to travel it again. For our battalion a cloud hung over this trip when Clare soldier, Private Gary Maloney, lost his leg below the knee after a landmine exploded while a unit was in the process of making a roadway safe for use. Five of our other personnel were injured in the incident though not as seriously.

'It was then that Dermot's leadership was really shown. We were all traumatised by what happened and he was too but he couldn't allow himself the luxury of taking time to collect himself. He did all that needed to be done for the wounded soldiers and for their families. Although he felt deeply for them, I'd say no one was more shattered on a personal level; his resolution to continue as normal wherever possible was hugely courageous.

'Then over the next week he literally rallied the troops and got morale back up again so that we could all do what we had to do. It is only in a crisis when a true leader shows their mettle and we all saw at that stage just how good a leader he was. He did all the big things and a whole myriad of small things to lift everybody back up after such a devastating blow.'

New ventures

After he was appointed Chief of Staff Dermot's engagement with peacekeeping moved on to another level. His previous experience was uppermost in his mind:

'I was responsible for the redeployment of Irish troops in Chad. It was not something I entered into lightly – knowing the risk for the Irish troops involved.'

Dermot's contacts in conflict zones would become very useful when an Irish national was taken hostage when working with a development agency. A laybrinth of Irish government departments were involved:

'The hostage was released eventually. The nation was happy. Nobody knew anything about my role which was as it should be but it was a great thrill when we got the happy outcome. It was very satisfying but involved many hours of work behind the scenes.'

Following in his father's footsteps

Leaning over the banisters in heaven Dermot Earley would have been proud to see his son Dermot Jnr continue the family tradition in autumn 2013: 'The Irish army has a rich history of peacekeeping. It is a role we are very familiar with. We had a continuous battalion in the Lebanon for 22 years. I had heard all the stories of these great places and it was a wonderful to become part of that history myself. But to make it even more special Dad had been the Battalion Commander over there in 1997 so from that point of view I really wanted to be part of that history. Following Dad's history was emotional.'

It was almost inevitable that he should have chosen to follow his father to this troubled spot: 'I grew up in Kildare on the edge of the Curragh. There is a huge involvement of the army. The fact that my father was in the army and would come home every evening and would tell stories of doing something different I knew then what I wanted to do. Moving to New York when Dad served with the UN, I could see the joy he took out of it all and since I came back from America aged 14, I said: "'Yeah, the army that's what I want to do too."'

Dermot Jnr had delayed volunteering for service in Lebanon: 'With the way the game has gone I had only once volunteered to go on peacekeeping mission in Bosnia in 2004-5. I would go to an American base and run on an American football field with rugby posts. I used to practise every day. When Dad was serving in Lebanon he would run and bounce a ball most mornings despite the risk of sniper fire. People can say it's almost copybook. It's just how much he enjoyed it. I could see how much he got out of it. It was obvious, so little wonder I wanted to follow.

'It was a conscious decision not to volunteer earlier than this. Back in the day it was possible to volunteer for six months and then came straight back on the county team. Anthony Rainbow had a few trips abroad with the army while he was still playing for Kildare but now managers want these players back training in January or even beforehand. As a player I wanted to do that myself especially as I got older when I could see the end of my football career in sight. I always believed there would be plenty of time when I hung my boots and that's when I volunteered.

'It came just after I announced my retirement from intercounty football so that was great help in easing the transition from county footballer to ex-county footballer. When you are playing at the highest level you have to be very selfish whereas in Lebanon you need to be selfless and that adjustment has been very rewarding. Mind you, I am looking forward to playing club football again with Sarsfields, injuries permitting.'

On a break home from his tour for his sister's Paula's wedding in February 2014, Dermot had reason to marvel that the professional approach to inter-county level had already risen another notch even in the few months since his retirement:

'I have met a couple of the lads since I came home and they were hugely positive. Kieran McGeeney brought a level of professionalism to Kildare we had never seen but Jason Ryan brought us another step forward. I was talking to the boys and they told me that they can now order their food for the week from the team nutritionist so that they can know what they are eating and that level of detail is something I would never have thought of.'

He did though bring his football interest with him overseas: 'One of our roles is to go to local schools and orphanages. I sometimes bring a GAA element. They've been instructed on how to kick a point and how to strike a sliotar and have been introduced to soccer and rugby as well. Gaelic games are unique to Ireland so when we go abroad we bring that with us and when you see them hopping a ball or doing a solo run it is very fulfilling. To spend a day doing that is a great day and if I can use it to improve relations with the locals it is a great feeling.

The Lebanese are a very resilient people. Sport is a massive part of the culture. They are all crazy about the Premier League. Every village I go to I see a soccer pitch.

'Our role is to monitor, support and assist. We monitor the blue line – the border between Lebanon and Israel. My specific role is as the link between the military and the civil population and to try and improve relations between the two.'

The Irish are part of a larger multinational force: 'The conflict goes back a long time. There's 37 nations involved in the peacekeeping project. From an Irish point of view when we went back to Lebanon the locals were delighted because of the way we can get on with people – which is why we are such good peacekeepers.

'It was an eye-opener to see the legacy of conflict. It's a life experience. We can give out about our country and makes you really appreciate how great a country we are and how great a people we are. You miss home and are in a different world and a different part of the world – so of course it's tough but I volunteered to go.'

Four years on after his father's death Dermot Jnr has had some time to try and appraise his father's career: 'Since Dad passed the thing that most colleagues say to me that what they miss most about him is his leadership.'

10

Hello Darkness My Old Friend

HAPPINESS is not having what you want but wanting what you have. For 61 years of his life Dermot Earley was a happy man.

When he died in June 2010 from a rapid degenerative condition Creutzfeldt-Jakob disease, his death and funeral were lead items on the RTE news. Over 5000 people went on Facebook to comment on his passing. He was aged 62. He had retired from the Defence Forces weeks before his death although he was not due to stand down until the following spring.

Less than two months before his death, Dermot was presented with the Distinguished Service Medal by the then Taoiseach Brian Cowen. It was to be his final public appearance. His son, Dermot, carries on his name. He believes that his father had some understanding of the significance of the occasion: 'He knew something was happening, of course, and I think he was sad that he realised that this might be the last time that he would wear the uniform.'

Dermot Jnr began to notice problems with his father in 2009: 'I suppose the first time we noticed something was wrong with Dad was that September. He had lost a bit of weight. Being in the job he was, and being the health-conscious man he was and looking after his diet, we did not wonder about that too much.

'But there were other things that drew our attention. He was having difficulty leaving the room or even finding the door; simple things like that. At the same time he was perfectly capable of having a strong conversation with you and from my point of view was still very able to tell me where I was going wrong in the football.

'Unfortunately though, the little things started to get bigger. January brought the diagnosis. He quickly went from being this larger than life individual who was so strong both physically and mentally to someone you can see actually getting worse and worse each week, to the point where he wasn't able to speak properly and get his words across.

'One of the complications was that a lot of people had many misunderstandings about his illness. Just two weeks ago somebody asked me: did he get it from eating something when he was on overseas duty? They did not understand that it was a degenerative brain condition and not something you get from eating contaminated food.

'The one thing he kept was his smile. I knew there were times when he was aware he wasn't well and that it was tough for him but the man he was always had the smile. A lot of people had come to the house in the last few months. On one occasion Micheál Ó Muicheartaigh called when Dad wasn't really communicating at all but Micheál sat down beside him and started talking. I was in the kitchen watching them and I saw Dad brightening up as he recognised the voice. It was a nice moment.'

A rumour spread like wildfire through media outlets that Dermot died a day before he actually did – though unlike the case of Ger Loughnane when he became ill the following year, whose death was erroneously reported by a national newspaper at the cost of great trauma for his family, nobody went public about the story.

For Dermot's wife Mary it was naturally a tough time: 'In the end he didn't know who he was or what he was. You had to bring him with you and mind him and steer him. That was the horrible part of it. I don't think I cried at his funeral. It comes later and the reality of it sets in two months later and then you begin to think about it and you ask what happened?'

Mary's Boy Child

His father's presence is still very real to Dermot Jnr: 'It was great to have someone who had done it and made the right decisions and was able to give me that knowledge so I was nothing but proud to have the name of Dermot Earley.

'I would have spoken to him before matches and also after matches and he would always say, "Well done, but just a couple of things," and when he went and analysed the game and how I played, he was always right. I know when I started playing for Kildare there were some who worried that my name would be a disadvantage because people would say: you were never the player your father was. But I was delighted to be called after him and even more so now that he is not with us any more.

'I have to be grateful for the man he was and how much I learned from him. I'll always be very grateful he was my father. The values that were dear to Dad in sport were sportsmanship, discipline and teamwork. Thankfully, my mother is a very strong woman. Everybody knows that my father was a huge influence but my Mam is as well. She is a huge GAA supporter and a very good analyst.

'My parents were the most important people in my life and they thought me to face every challenge. They always encouraged me to remain positive despite setbacks. Your family will always be there for you. Dad always stressed the importance of an education, writing down your goals, how to recover from setbacks and keeping leisure time active.'

My brother's keeper

For Paul Earley it was a turbulent time: 'We were always close. I had moved to Kildare and got into club management. We got to the county final and ended up playing Sarsfields with Dermot as selector and David and Dermot Jnr having starring roles. They won but Dermot came in to our dressing-room and was very emotional and was very supportive of me. The problem was that we drew Sarsfields three years-in-a-row and it was at once always funny but slightly strained after the draw was made.

'In April or May 2009, I got a call from Seamus Hayden and he asked me: "Is the big fella okay?" There was a rumour out there that he had Motor Neuron disease. Two of the Roscommon team that had won the All-Ireland under-21 title in 1966 with Dermot had acquired the condition. I hadn't spoken to Dermot in a few weeks at that stage so I rang him. He laughed heartily. He told me he was fit as ever and said: "Tell Hayden I will take him on anywhere anytime if he wants to."

'That September though Dermot Jnr rang me to say they were a bit concerned about him because he was doing small things like putting the milk back into the press rather than the fridge. I went to see him and his body language was not good though he was still very articulate. He seemed to have gone in on himself. I could sense something was not right and that he wasn't letting something out.

'I was going down to Roscommon shortly afterwards to spend the day with my mother and asked him to join me. He was very quiet in the car on the way down, which was very unusual. He didn't initiate any conversation. It was all left to me.

'When we got to our mother's house he normally would have sat down in the chair and chatted but he was up making the tea and doing all the small jobs my mother always did. Looking back now, I think he was obviously trying to challenge himself to do simple tasks.

'My mother knew immediately there was something wrong. We brought her to Knock and headed to Ballyhaunis for lunch. When we came out I went to open the door of the driver's seat and got a bit of a shock because he was there on my shoulder to get ready to sit in the driver's seat and I said: "No, you're over the other side.' He said: "Oh yeah." His behaviour had changed and he was much quieter so the signs were there.

'There had been a lot of stress in the job at the time. His two deputies had not been replaced because of the embargo on recruitment in the Defence Forces and he was doing three jobs. The economic crash had happened and they brought cutbacks everywhere. The biggest thing for him was the army closures, which is a very emotional issue for all the personnel involved, and he felt their pain and frustration very keenly. Telling army people and their families that they had to uproot their lives and move to another army base took a lot out of him because he knew exactly how upsetting it was for all those concerned and their families. I spoke to a consultant I knew and he said Dermot's symptoms were consistent with the early stages of Alzheimer's but sometimes the same symptoms can be the same for someone with serious stress. I hoped it was just stress.

'Shortly after this my wife Mairead was diagnosed with a serious condition so I was kind of on autopilot. Fortunately, she has made a full recovery but she had a tough time for six or seven months. At that stage it was very difficult to juggle everything as I was trying to manage my business and my two girls were studying for their Junior Cert and Daniel was only six.

'Dermot took time off work. My mother rang me when she heard this and asked what was wrong because she said Dermot was never sick nor took time off. I think she knew intuitively that he was seriously ill and was not going to recover. When the diagnosis came she was very strong but it was very hard on her. The hardest thing for any parent is to bury your child and she had to do that. When she died in 2013, Dermot was not there. That's not the way things are supposed to be.

'After the diagnosis I have three really happy memories. The first was early on and although he was down and knew time was running out and he was not going to achieve all the things he wanted to do, we chatted for half an hour and it was the most open conversation I ever had with him. I told him exactly what I thought of him and how much he meant to me. He told me some of the sensitive things he had been involved in the army that I never knew about and gave me a real insight into the importance of his work.

'As things started to deteriorate he came out to visit our house and sat down beside my son Daniel and I will never forget watching them playing together.

'When he got worse I went to visit him in the Hospice when he wasn't really communicating. When I came in and sat down he winked at me. Paula was there at the time and she said: "Did you see that?"

'He took a turn on the Sunday before he died and I spent the next few days with him and the rest of his family until he took his last breath and I am so glad I was there at the end. The army chaplains and the Hospice staff were incredible.'

A daughter's love

When Robert Kennedy was assassinated in 1968, his brother Ted said at the funeral that he, 'need not be enlarged in death beyond what he was in life but to be remembered simply as a good and decent man who saw wrong and tried to right it, saw suffering and tried to heal it.'

Anne-Marie Earley was keen that the family would not go overboard but simply reflect the kind of man their father was: 'We prepared a memorial card and handed it out at his funeral it outlined the five points of Dad's Plan for Life.

1. Enjoy time with my family.

2. Give the best to my work.

3. Give back to my community.

4. Spend my leisure time well.

5. Make time for God in my life.'

Later Dermot Jnr would be struck at the speed at which dreams can be shattered and how close the veil between life and death is as tragedy swoops like a hawk flying down from the sky, a fearsome beast, ferocious as it ripped and shred and tore, attacking all it saw:

'On the morning of Dad's removal as we were having our breakfast, Mickey Harte called to express his sympathies. As he shared tea and toast with us I never dreamt then that just seven months later my mother would end up making the journey to Tyrone to offer words of condolence to Mickey after the horrific murder of his much loved daughter, Mikaela.'

Enda Kenny was among one of many people to pay tribute to his fellow Connacht man: 'Dermot Earley was, I believe, one of the most iconic Chiefs of Staff of the Defence Forces since Michael Collins.'

The army did a magnificent job (Dermot himself would have said 'mighty') at organising the funeral, with Dermot's great friend John Courtney orchestrating all the arrangements. The two men had played against each other in the 1979 League final, the one National honour at senior level that Dermot had won. Before that match the two men had made a pact that the winner and his wife would take the loser and his wife out to dinner the week after the game. After the final whistle the first person to congratulate Earley was Cork's John Courtney who also took the opportunity to remind him about their dinner date.

Among the army personnel on duty outside the Church marshalling the huge crowd was Sue Ramsbottom, the Laois star who is one of the greatest ladies' footballers of all time. She and Dermot had formed an informal mutual admiration society.

The congregation sitting in the Church with shafts of silver light descending from the highest windows included the great and the good of the army, the GAA and the world of politics and the media. Great opponents of the past like Eoin Bomber Liston were there to pay their respects.

The members of the 1980 Roscommon team were reunited to mourn a fallen comrade outside the Church. In 1992 I had asked Dermot how he wanted to be remembered. He replied: 'As a good man.' Gay Sheeran remarked: 'It was one of those rare occasions when Dermot was wrong. He wasn't a good man. He was a great man.'

Before the funeral Mass began David Martin emerged on the altar and sang a spine-tingling version of *The West's Awake*. His song set the tone for the funeral which was of a celebration of a rich life well lived. It was only towards the very end of the Mass that the tone changed when two of Dermot's children made short but powerful contributions. David's role was primarily to thank all who had given support had such a difficult time. When Paula spoke though about her father her anguish and devastation were clearly evident and the congregation were immediately reminded of the family's heartbreak. The ache of it filled the Church and friends felt sorry not for themelves but for the family Dermot had loved so much. Even when they could not cry the pain was evident behind the eyes, in the tautness in the throat and the tightening of the rib cage.

As the coffin was lowered the mourners exhaled deeply. Eyes began to moisten and a wave of sadness washed over the cemetery.

Tough choice

To adapt George Bernard Shaw, Gaelic football was not a brief candle to Dermot but a splendid torch which he had got hold of and wanted to make it burn as brightly as possible before handing it on to future generations. On the day his father was buried, the family home like a tomb with the stone rolled over the top, muted and enclosed in grief, Dermot Junior faced a dilemma. Should he play for Kildare that evening in an important Qualifier against Antrim?

'I suppose it's one of those things that maybe people might not understand or people might say you should have been at home with your family. Football in our house is a massive part of our lives. After all, it's the family that allows the person to go and make the commitment and go to all that training and miss out on all the other things they could be doing together. The love is there, the family want the player to succeed, and they allow them to do that stuff. All that week I knew the match was coming. My Dad passed on Wednesday and I sat down and I talked to Mam and my brothers and sisters and I didn't want anything extra to change. There was enough already changing.

'At the same time I was conscious of the funeral and I felt that Dad would have wanted me to play. He knew how much it meant to me and he would have wanted me to go out there and give it my best. That's exactly what he said to me every time I played a match, go out and give it your best. It's the same thing I said going out to play against Antrim. But that night I went home, went up to my parents' house, my Mam's house, and a lot of things go through your head. And I suppose for maybe that hour and a half of the game, I was able to concentrate on that match and have that release. But again it's not something that requires any extra praise. Great loss happens to people every day.'

Up the Rossies

For Dermot Jnr his father's funeral was a very forceful reminder of the place of Roscommon in the family history: There were many times I went to Roscommon with him for training when I was a boy. He would recall past contests and I would say: "I know Dad, you told me last week." I suppose though over the years we kind of forgot just how big a deal he was in Roscommon.

'When it came to his removal there was a constant flow of people. It was something I will never forget to see the amount of people who wanted to say goodbye to him. We found it overwhelming. It seemed as if all of Roscommon had come to pay its respects at the funeral as well as representatives of the wider GAA family. Dad was given a military funeral, which is a fairly sombre event. As his coffin was laid in to the ground and after the last post was played and everyone was quiet I think it was Gay Sheeran who shouted out: "Up the Rossies." It brought a little smile to people at what was a very tough time.

'He was so proud of where he was from. To the people of Roscommon he was a hero. To me he was just a father. Sometimes we forgot how much he meant to people. We received a great many letters of support, particularly from people who never knew him, and that meant a lot.

'Dad would have had great anticipation before Roscommon's famous Connacht final win over Sligo shortly after his death. He would have kicked every ball during the game and, at the end, he would have had a big smile on his face. I think his spirit was all around Castlebar that day.'

As fate would have it the sporting Gods decreed that Roscommon and Kildare both played their All-Ireland quarter-finals the same day in Croke Park The rich wells of sentiment plays a huge part in every corner of the GAA. Despite their tingles of anticipation before the match fans recalled absent friends: 'I did not see it myself but I was told afterwards that during the first game Roscommon's defeat to Cork, a huge banner in the crowd read "Earley – 8 – Legend, 1948-2010." Despite the rain many of the Rossies hung around to cheer me and Kildare on as a tribute to Dad. He would have meant so much to them and it was their way of paying their respects. It was a nice gesture and it meant a lot.'

The unique power of the GAA is its capacity to lift the shadows off the hearts of even its most troubled fans. Like us all the rain has fallen on the Earleys but that was a day to be happy. Paul Earley believes that one of Dermot's legacies is a special closeness between Kildare and Roscommon fans: 'I take immense pleasure in all of Roscommon's achievements. I especially recall Roscommon's provincial senior success in 2001, after a 10-year barren period. My twin girls, who were seven at the time, never saw their dad as animated at a game, so much so that one of them was thrown in the air (with great skill and accuracy) when Gerry Lohan scored the famous goal to win the game in injury-time.

'Instilling a love for your home county in your children isn't always easy, but significant victories help in a big way. The famous qualifier game in 2003 in Portlaoise sticks in my mind, not just because it was an enthralling game and because of Frankie Dolan's magnificent 13 points, but it was the day when my twins became true supporters of the "Primrose and Blue". I know this because at half-time in extra time, the Lilywhite jerseys were taken off to reveal the Roscommon jersey underneath.

'Fast forward 10 years and we now have the "half and half jersey", which we have seen a few Roscommon people wear in Croke Park to show their support for Dermot Jnr., on those days when both Roscommon and Kildare were playing.'

Dermot Junior never ceases to be amazed by the attitude people in Roscommon have for his father: 'The support we got from all over Ireland, but especially from the people of Roscommon, was unbelievable and still is. I've been down there a number of times for different events and any time his name is mentioned the place goes silent. It's unbelievable to see it. If there was a scale invented to measure passion for football and for your county, Roscommon would be off the charts.

'When I was young, we used to go down to Hyde Park training with Dad all the time. You don't appreciate the magnitude of it. And then the fact we were living in Kildare, you forget almost how much he meant. But even that day, my family and sisters were in the stand and the amount of Roscommon people that went up to them was incredible. It was very special.

'Of course the fact that Kildare won was a consolation. I hoped to play in the semi-final. With the benefit of hindsight I was probably lying to myself. The morning of the Down game I went for a fitness test and could run a straight line as well as at any stage in his career, but turning was a different story.

'Obviously it's hard when you go so far in summer and it would be special to win an All-Ireland at any time, but it would have been so special to have won one the year my father died – especially because he never won one.'

The Keane Edge

Dermot died within a short time of rugby legend Moss Keane. The two had become friends after attending a charity auction for GOAL in 1979. Dermot donated the jersey he had worn in the League final which raised £100. He was not sure if he should feel complimented with the price, or insulted when the buyer Terry Rodgers told him: 'My father was from Roscommon but thanks be to God he got out early.'

Moss brought the house down when he told how Ireland had lost narrowly to Wales in Cardiff Arms Park earlier in the year despite a breath-taking performance by Tony Ward. The game is best remembered though for Ireland's fullback and future Tánaiste Dick

Spring dropping a ball, which let Wales in for a soft try and earning Spring the nickname 'Butterfingers' on *Scrap Saturday*. In his own distinctive style Moss held up a plastic bag and recalled how he had gone into the Welsh dressing room after the game to swop jerseys with Allan Martin the Welsh forward. On his way out big Moss remembered that Martin had not been a good man to buy a round of drinks on the Lions tour, so he went back inside and 'borrowed' Martin's tracksuit while he was in the shower, to compensate for all the drinks Keane had bought him on the Lions tour.

He also said you have to pick your fights. To illustrate he recalled how he was once selected to play for the Welsh Barbarians against a touring South Africa team. The game turned violent, with numerous bouts of fisticuffs. At one stage 29 of the players on the field were fighting ferociously. Moss was the sole non-combatant. Asked later why he was so uncharacteristically Gandhian Moss replied: 'I might die for Ireland but I'm fu**ed if I'm going to die for Wales.'

Moss also spoke about driving from Dublin for a match in Tralee with Dick Spring. The two boys always shortened the journey by doing the crossword from *The Irish Times*. Moss proudly held the record for getting the crossword done before they got to Kildare. On this day though Spring was on fire and answering every question. Spring was driving that day and Moss noticed that he was not pushing his foot on the pedal as hard as they approached Kildare, with a new record in sight. Moss called out a clue: 'Postman loses mail.'

Spring scratched his head and observed: 'That should be easy to do.' He repeated the clue a number of times. Finally he asked: 'How many letters?'

Moss gleefully replied: 'Every fu**ing one of them!'

A Warrior Prince

Dermot's true epitaph will be written in the memory of his people. A year after his death an exhibition entitled 'Dermot Earley – Leader and Legend' opened in the GAA Museum in Croke Park from his life as a hugely successful Gaelic footballer and his distinguished military career in the Irish Defence Forces. The same year the people of Gorthaganny erected a magnificent life-size memorial in his honour. Having made Dermot the first official free citizen of County Roscommon at a civic reception given in his honour at the County Council chamber in 2009 Roscommon County Council established their Dermot Earley Bursary which is an annual scheme, which provides two Sports scholarships, intended for persons of outstanding sporting ability.

Before he too was sadly taken so suddenly Paidí Ó Sé honoured Dermot's memory at his annual football tournament in Ventry. The Earley family were not given a chance to feel sad as Paidí's vast catalogue of stories from his career were recalled with gusto. He told them of the day a young Kerry team arrived on the train the day before the 1975 All-Ireland final – as Páidí rushed off and was greeted by a photogapher who asked him if he knew where the senior footballers were. 'The Kerry senior team', in case Páidí did not know what he meant.

'Back there somewhere', Páidí mischeviously replied.

Before the 1984 All-Ireland Páidí extended his hand to shake Dublin's Joe McNally's hand but Big Joe raced forward and shouldered him at pace knocking him on his behind. Páidí picked his moment for retribution. During the National Anthem when everyone's eyes were elsewhere he kicked Joe in the backside and knocked him over. Páidí had the last laugh as he held McNally scoreless and the Dublin forward was substituted.

As Mary Earley acknowledged: 'It was a lovely tribute from Paidí and one we all appreciated.'

For his part Dermot's admiration of the Kerry star was fulsome: 'Páidí was a bit of a rogue in the best and nicest sense of the term. I had a few good evenings with him in my time. He would come out with the most incredible stories. You wouldn't always be sure if they were true but you would always be entertained. He adds to the gaiety of the nation.'

Dunne Deal

Charlie Finneran's award-winning Derryglad Folk Museum in Curraghboy in South Roscommon is a repository of secrets and dreams. It is a unique theatre of Irish social history, stirring abiding memories in its visitors who recall bygone days of horse-drawn machinery and homemade butter making and evoking reminiscences of a different time. It shows how our destiny as a nation was crossed, matted as fibres long inwrought into the fabric of other stories, like our national games. Its sports section holds the ultimate memorabilia for any Roscommon fan, a copy of the 1944 All-Ireland programme.

On the second anniversary of his death, thanks to the generousity of Finbarr Feely and Feelystone in Boyle a memorial stone was unveiled in Dermot's memory at the museum. Given his own interest in history Dermot had expressed a wish to present his own jersey to the museum, but sadly never got to make the journey so the family came that day to make the presentation in a poignant ceremony.

The special guest was RTE's Eileen Dunne who recalled that her father, the late Mick Dunne, had a very close relationship with Dermot and spoke about how he had been captivated by a tour of the UN buildings in New York given by Dermot while he was working there: 'I met him on a few occasions myself and was struck by his fantastic oratory skills and I often thought how impressive it was that the country had a Chief of Staff of the Defence Forces of his calibre. Some say maybe one day he would have been President and what a wonderful one he would have been.'

Anne-Marie Earley - who showed herself to be a real keeper of her father's flame, ably filled in any gaps in Eileen's knowledge on the day.

Mr. President?

When I questioned Dermot about the rumour that he was being considered as a candidate for the presidency he laughed and told me a fable about politics:

'While walking down the street one day a female head of state is tragically hit by a car and dies. Her soul arrives in heaven and is met by St Peter at the entrance.

"Welcome to Heaven," said St Peter. "Before you settle in, it seems there is a problem. We seldom see a high official around these parts, you see, so we're not sure what to do with you."

"No problem, just let me in," says the lady.

"Well, I'd like to but I have orders from higher up. What'll we do is have your spend one day in Hell and one in Heaven. Then you can choose where to spend eternity."

"Really, I've made up in my mind. I want to be in Heaven", says the head of state.

"I'm sorry but we have our rules." And with that, St Peter escorts her to the elevator and she goes down, down, down to Hell. The doors opened and she found herself in the middle of a golf course. In the distance is a club and standing in front of it are all her friends and the politicians who had worked with her. Everyone is very happy and in evening dress. They greet her, hug her, and reminisce about the good times they had while getting rich at the expense of the people. They play a friendly game of golf and then dine on lobster. Also present is the Devil, who really is a very friendly guy who has a good time dancing and telling jokes. They are having such a good time that, before she realises it, it is time to go. Every one gave her a big hug and waves while the elevator rises. The elevator goes up, up, up and reopens on Heaven where St Peter is waiting for her.

"Now it's time to visit Heaven." So 24 hours pass with the head of state joining a large number of contented souls moving from cloud to cloud, playing the harp and singing. Before she realises it, the 24 hours have gone by and St Peter returns: "Well then, you've spent a day in Hell and another in Heaven. Now choose your eternal destination."

She reflects for a minute, then the head of state answers, "Well, I would never have expected it. I mean Heaven has been delightful, but I think I would be better off in Hell."

So Saint Peter escorts her to the elevator and she goes down, down, down to hell. The doors of the elevator open and she is in the middle of a barren land covered with garbage. She sees all her friends, dressed in rags, picking up the trash and putting it in bags. The Devil comes over to her and lays his arm on her neck.

"I don't understand," stammers the head of state, "Yesterday I was here and everyone was on the golf course and club and we ate lobster and caviar and danced and had a great time. Now it is a wasteland full of garbage and my friends look miserable."

'The Devil looks at her, smiles and says: "Yesterday we were campaigning. Today you voted for us!"

'There are many great people in politics but I am not sure I have all the qualities that are needed to be a success in the political realm. I am not sure I would want to have all those qualities.'

Gone but not Forgotten

An enduring memorial to Dermot is the 'Dermot Earley Youth Leadership Initiative'. This unique programme honours one of Ireland's greatest ever leaders, and is brought together by the National University of Ireland, Galway, Foróige, and the GAA. Lively and interactive, the programme aims to inspire a new generation to achieve their full leadership potential both on and off the field of play.

It will offer 45 young GAA club members, 15 each from counties Roscommon, Kildare, and Galway, the opportunity to develop and explore their leadership skills through a programme that evokes and honours the values Dermot epitomised. Speaking on behalf of the Earley family, Dermot Jnr, said: 'Enabling young people to achieve their full potential was something my father was passionate about. We are delighted to give our support to this initiative and look forward to the positive influence these young leaders will have on their GAA clubs, their communities and beyond.'

The lucky participants, who must be between 15- to 18-years-old, will explore all elements of leadership before being asked to put their skills to work in their own clubs, communities, or schools. The course involves 50 instructional hours. It commenced in Croke Park on Saturday, October 26 2013, where everyone got a feel for the programme before taking in the International Rules match against Australia in the famed stadium. To add an extra layer of poignancy the Ireland team was managed by Dermot's brother Paul. Following the initial gathering in Croke Park, all subsequent sessions took place in the participants' own county and was delivered by GAA and Foróige volunteers who had received specific training in NUIG. The course is part-time in nature and is delivered in the evenings and at weekends through a timetable that will avoid interference with school and other educational or sporting commitments. Those who complete all three modules will be eligible to graduate from NUIG with a Foundation Certificate in Youth Leadership and Community Action.

In May 2014 things came the full circle when as part of her Dermot Earley Leadership Initiative Edel Coffey from the Michael Glaveys club organised a *This Is Your Life* style tribute to Dermot.

All-Ireland winning manager Jim Gavin, himself a former member of the Defence Forces, spoke publicly in 2014 about the way in which Dermot Earley had been a significant influence in his philosophy of leadership. In particular he stressed that he had been particularly taken on Dermot's emphasis on being the best that you can be.

The Empty Chair at the Christmas Table

Like his father before him Dermot Junior had a glittering career but unlike his Dad injury forced him to retire prematurely in 2013 after a lengthy struggle with injury, or more accurately injuries: 'In 2010 I jarred my knee in an early-season training and turned on it in a league game against Laois, a moment that caused me to tear 90 per cent of the cruciate ligament. I was told I'd need an operation eventually, but I may be able to keep playing. It depended on how strong my quads and other muscles were to stabilise the knee. So I kept going.

'The doctor said I would have to tone it down about 10 per cent but in Championship instinct takes over. And I remember thinking against Leitrim when I came down from the throw in at the start of the second half, the last bit of the ligament is gone and it's completely torn. I played on for a while that day and in the rest of the qualifiers I had no problems. There were times when I would get a dart of pain but it went away again. If you were in the same boat, then you'd do in the same thing. Any footballer would keep going unless his leg was hanging off. I don't want it to sound like I'm delighted I came through some pain barrier and it makes me unique. I'm not.

'My knee had little holding it together. But I knew the minute I went to launch a long ball into the Kildare full-forward line early on in the quarterfinal against Meath that I was in big trouble. I got up thinking: "I've been down before and carried on." But this time I just couldn't play with a snapped cruciate. Tests later revealed my knee bones had slid out of place as they had in the games against Derry and Monaghan, but this time they never slid back. The real pain came from missing the games themselves.'

According to conventional wisdom time heals all wounds. That has not been the experience of Dermot Jnr: 'Its been tough on all of us – my Mam most of all. Each of us probably experience Dad's passing in different ways. When Paula and Anne Marie got married, Dad was not there and I am sure they felt his absence keenly. I guess for me one of the toughest things, and it's still tough, is not having him there to ask about stuff. And it's not even about football, it's other things as well. For instance, a few months after he died I was doing some work and my first thought was I must ask Dad what he thinks of this. Then I realised he was gone and at moments like that the reality hits me. We used to talk a lot about football before games and a lot after and that's something I have missed.

'Every Christmas Dad would give out the Christmas presents when we came home for Mass with a big smile on his face. The last few Christmasses he hasn't been there for that and it may seem a small thing but it's a very big thing for me.'

This experience has given Dermot a new understanding of Christmas: 'My mother does all she can to make Christmas a happy event despite the sadness we all feel about Dad's absence. Dad always said Christmas was a time to remember absent friends and now I know what he meant.'

The long goodbye

For each of the six Earley children it has been a profound adjustment since their father died. He was their hero, their role model, their mentor, their friend, their idol, their teacher, sometimes their accomplice in mischief, and the one who gave them their values. At first they were not sure if they could survive properly without him.

Laughter was but a fading memory. Tears were inadequate vehicles for their grief. Their mother had lost not just a husband but a large part of her own self. Their tower of strength had crumbled. They briefly wondered if they could ever love again but they soon learned that love can live long after death. It is a second time love, like a summer shower, the leaves having retained the rain, rain on the unsuspecting head as though it had rained again.

It might have been a depressing story. In fact it is quite the opposite. In sessions of sweet silent thought they have come to understand that Dermot's love, like soft summer rain, can nourish from above, drenching his family with a soaking joy.

Tenebrae Cedant Luci – Let darkness yield to light.

Acknowledgements

THANKS to Mary Earley and all the Earley family for their generous support for this book.

I am greatly honoured that Dermot Earley Junior agreed to write the foreword for the book. Nobody else could have carried off the seemingly impossible task of taking on his father's name with such amazing grace. The greatest compliment I could pay him is to say he is his father's son.

Thanks to Paul Earley for his friendship down the years and his willingness to always give a practical hand.

I am grateful to PJ Cunningham and all at Ballpoint Press for backing this idea so enthusiastically from day one. In fact in 2005 PJ was the main mover in Dermot receiving the MBNA Kick Fada Hall of Fame.

My deepest gratitude to John Boyle, the Earley family, Aidan Farrell, Adam and Harry Minogue, Teresa Scally, Eibhlin Sharkey and the Defence Forces for their help with photos for this book.

Thanks to Paddy Joe Burke, Tom Carr, Tony Conboy, Eileen Dunne, Gerry Hegarty, Johnny Hughes, Harry Keegan, Seán Kilbride, T.J. Kilgallon, Pat Lindsay, Kevin McStay, Jimmy Magee, Barnes Murphy, Danny Murray, John O'Mahony, Mickey and Mary Quinn, Sue Ramsbottom, Colin Regan, Gay Sheeran and Brian Talty for their insights.

My special thanks to the great Seamus Hayden for his unwavering friendship and his willingness to always give a helping hand.

Particular thanks too to GAA Communications Director Alan Milton for his support.

Thanks to Joe Coyle for his expertise and professionalism.

Fiona Maher has been much in my thoughts as this book was written. Her much-loved brother, Gerard, will never be forgotten.

2014 has seen some events, which Dermot would have liked to acknowledge had he been still with us. In February his great friend Brian Carthy was honoured with the Hall of Fame award in the GAA's prestigious McNamee awards – which Dermot would have seen as a fitting tribute to Brian's lifetime of dedicated service to the GAA. He would also have been happy to see another Roscommon man, Brendan Hynes, win a McNamee award for his outstanding service to St Brigid's as a photographer.

Sadly one of the legends of Roscommon and Connacht football, Brendan Lynch, left us. I am sure that Dermot has already discovered that heaven has become much more interesting with Brendan's presence. Tragically Brian Donnelly was taken from us much, much too soon. His loss to his family, to the hurling community in Four Roads, and to the wider GAA family in Roscommon is incalculable.

After a glittering career and years of distinguished service to Kildare Johnny Doyle retired from intercounty football. We will not see his like again.

Thanks to Shannonside radio for their interest in the Dermot Earley story especially Martin Howard, Mike Mulvihill and Colm Gallagher.

Special thanks to Jane Welch for her kindness and goodness.

Index